D1345903

A Grand Experiment

The CONSTITUTION at

·200·

Douglass Greybill Adair (1912–1968)

Born in New York City, Douglass Adair grew up in Birmingham and Mobile, Alabama. He majored in English at the University of the South in Sewanee and took an M.A. at Harvard and his Ph.D. at Yale. After teaching at Princeton, he joined the faculty of the College of William and Mary in 1946 and became editor of the *William and Mary Quarterly.* From 1955 until his death, he was professor of history at the Claremont Graduate School. A scholar of great reputation, a skilled editor, and an inspirational teacher, he was a lover of his discipline and a friend to all who practiced it.

A Grand Experiment

The CONSTITUTION at

·200·

Essays from the Douglass Adair Symposia

Edited by
John Allphin Moore, Jr.
and
John E. Murphy

♦

SR Scholarly Resources Inc.
Wilmington, Delaware

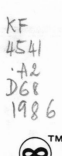

The paper used in this publication meets the minimum requirements of the American National Standard for permanence of paper for printed library materials, Z39.48, 1984.

Scholarly Resources Inc.
104 Greenhill Avenue
Wilmington, Delaware 19805-1897

Library of Congress Cataloging-in-Publication Data

Douglass Adair Symposia (1986 : California State
   Polytechnic University)
   A grand experiment.

   Includes index.
   1. United States—Constitutional history—Congresses.
I. Adair, Douglass.   II. Moore, John Allphin,
1940–   .   III. Murphy, John E. (John Edwin),
1940–   .   IV. Title.
KF4541.A2D68   1986   342.73′029   87-16754
                                347.30229
ISBN 0-8420-2289-9 (alk. paper)

Contents

Preface

Entering our third century as a nation, we should be reminded that this Republic began in the minds of its citizens as much as in the actions of a few revolutionaries. The great state documents of our history—the Declaration of Independence and the Constitution—were products of ideas that had circulated widely in the colonies and in the infant Revolutionary nation. That is, serious discourse about the nature of government and society in the modern age took place throughout the country.

The essays in this collection reflect in the best sense the aims and purposes of the Founders. During the winter and spring of 1986, scholars, public officials, teachers, lawyers, and students joined together in a dialogue about this country and its 200-year-old Constitution. This was the Douglass Adair Symposia, held at California State Polytechnic University, Pomona, and Pomona College in Claremont, and the presentations made and commentary offered have been preserved in this anthology. The participants also met with students, business and civic leaders, and the general public in a three-month-long consideration of the Constitution and its future.

It is with pride and excitement that we present these essays and commentaries as our contribution to the bicentennial celebration of the Constitution. The California State University, the largest system of senior higher education in the nation, prides itself on being a home for advanced scholarship and relevant teaching. We see as one of our missions the stimulation of dialogue about important issues among people of all walks of life. In addition, we were delighted to merge our efforts with members of the Claremont Colleges in an activity that combined the private and public sectors of the academy.

Those who made the symposia possible were the Exxon Educational Foundation, whose generosity was the underpinning of the project; the Associated Students, the Cal Poly Kellogg Unit Foundation, the School of Arts, and the President's Office at California State Polytechnic University, Pomona; the California Council for the Humanities; and the Johnson Lectureship, Pomona College.

Hugh O. La Bounty, president of California State Polytechnic University, Pomona, deserves special recognition for his leadership, support, and nourishment of the Douglass Adair Symposia. It was at his university that the project began and was administered. The outreach to the wider community of Southern California, we believe, has generated a renewed interest in the Constitution. This is, above all, what we had hoped from the beginning, for, in a republic, we all are in the business of government.

W. Ann Reynolds
Chancellor, California State University

Douglass Adair, the Constitution, and the American Experience

The decision by Professor Moore and his associates to dedicate this ambitious celebration of the bicentennial of the Constitution to the memory of Douglass Adair was most appropriate in at least two respects. In the first instance, it is the right moment to honor Adair for the profound and pervasive influence that he has had upon the scholarship of the Revolutionary and early national periods of American history. From Bernard Bailyn to Page Smith, this generation has had the benefit of a substantial number of first-class intellects who have concerned themselves with the Founders and the founding documents, but it would be difficult to identify any one person whose role has been so singular as Adair's in the development of what is currently the dominant interpretive school of scholarship.

The origin of what Robert Shalhope has called "the republican synthesis" can be traced to Adair's unpublished but much consulted doctoral dissertation in which he challenged the economic determinism of Charles Beard and the "Progressive historians." Adair cajoled and convinced a generation of scholars to acknowledge the fundamental role of ideas in the political life of the late eighteenth century. One needs only to read the acknowledgments in the most important studies published in the last fifteen or twenty years to appreciate the extent of his legacy.

As a historian, teacher, and editor, Adair was second to none in his respect for the unique reality of the past. Where others were quick to see analogy and parallel, he insisted on careful (as one of his former students, may I say, painfully careful) attention to the specificity of the event, the document, or the person. He had a musician's ear for particular or idiosyncratic intonation and had so attuned it to the eighteenth-century idiom that, as Trevor Colbourn has observed, "to some he seemed an eighteenth-century *philosophe* who had strayed into the twentieth century by some happy accident." And, as a *philosophe* should, Adair reminded us that, if Karl Marx had persuaded the late nineteenth and twentieth centuries to accord economic motivation primary status, the previous age had been much more convinced of the importance of political theory.

Because Beard had anchored his economic interpretation of the Constitution in the tenth *Federalist*, Adair began his challenge of the great Progressive with a revisit to that essay, first in his dissertation and later in two seminal articles. He was able to demonstrate that, far from using philosophy as a cover or rationalization to disguise economic motives, James Madison and his colleagues were serious in their belief "that politics may be reduced to a science" and in their conviction that the political experience of the past was a veritable mine from which knowledge and wisdom might be quarried.

Madison, by virtue of his education and reading, felt confident in directing his colleagues to consult experience as the only dependable teacher, but, as Adair was concerned to demonstrate, Madison's conception of experience was shaped by that same reading and education. The influence of the Scottish Enlightenment was particularly strong under the Witherspoon regime at Princeton, and the influence of Francis Hutcheson, and more especially David Hume, did much to color Madison's views of human nature and political society.

Madison's ideas about the nature of experience also had been conditioned by the tradition of seventeenth-century English republicanism. His references to the importance of civic virtue and to the ruinous influence of "faction" or party were not rhetorical exercises but serious preoccupations. Far from trying to create a government to safeguard the interests of the rich, as Beard would have it, Adair found Madison bent on designing a Newtonian mechanism that would neutralize "factions" and at the same time bring to leadership positions persons committed to seeking the public welfare, persons of broad vision and disinterested virtue.

While he often approached his research as an intellectual sleuth or cultural detective, Adair was not an antiquarian. Indeed, a second important reason for honoring him in a lecture series about the Constitution derives from his concept of the uses of history and scholarship. "History," he used to tell us, "is a conversation between the present and the past about the future." His concern was to make certain that the cross-generational conversation was coherent, and toward that end he thought it just as important to grasp the differences between past and present as to discern the similarities. In fact, it was in the exploration of those differences that he believed we might find the perspective, the insight, that could make our decisions about the future wiser and more productive.

All this is not to suggest that Adair was so "scientific" or "objective" that he did not find much in the lives and ideas of the Founders worthy of outright emulation. He did, after all, belong to the party of reason, and he hoped that the renewed interest in the

Founders that flowered in the postwar period would give birth to a new respect for ideas in the discussion of politics. John Gardner and Ralph Nader would be welcome in his study, as would the contributors to this volume, concerned as they are to seek the relevance of the ideas that informed the Constitution to our own time and circumstances. Douglass Adair subscribed to Thomas Jefferson's dictum that "eternal vigilance is the price of liberty," and he was fond of recalling Benjamin Franklin's response to a question put to him as he emerged from the final meeting of the Convention. "What kind of government is it to be?" his questioner asked. "A Republic," Franklin answered, "if you can keep it."

David L. Levering
Professor of History
California State Polytechnic
University, Pomona

Introduction

> It has been frequently remarked that it seems
> to have been reserved to the people of this
> country, by their conduct and example, to de-
> cide the important question, whether societies
> of men are really capable or not of establishing
> good government from reflection and choice,
> or whether they are forever destined to depend
> for their political constitutions on accident and
> force.
>
> —*The Federalist* No. 1

Alexander Hamilton's introductory essay to the most famous collection of writings on American politics reflects the optimism and audacity of eighteenth-century thought and, at the same time, challenges future generations to answer his question affirmatively. At the least we can say that the constitutional republic deeded to posterity continued to exist into its 200th birthday and thus provided for Americans an opportunity to celebrate a most important bicentennial. Some might say as well that the document the Founders concocted has performed very well, allowing the Republic to expand from 4 million inhabitants on the Atlantic coast of North America to a continental empire of a quarter of a billion, whose influence on the world probably is unmatched in history.

However, the Constitution, which is the fundamental guiding document of this Republic, is more revered than discussed. Except for those occasional moments when constitutional law is applied to intricate legal cases in our courts, this oldest written instrument of government is simply celebrated. There are no twentieth-century Anti-Federalists (opponents of the Constitution). Indeed, political debate in this country frequently is characterized by both sides of a controversy claiming sanction from the Constitution. It is secular Holy Writ for Americans. This undoubtedly would have pleased the Founders, but surely they would have us celebrate such an extraordinary birthday by probing the concerns, political views, and solutions upon which they cogitated two centuries ago and consider how these measure up to the issues, problems, and challenges of our own time. This is not to suggest some crude relativist critique of the Constitution but rather a careful examination of the Constitution's meaning and role in the course of the American experiment.

In addition, if we take seriously Hamilton's charge, then it may be incumbent upon us to determine whether or not we have as a nation, by our conduct and example, continued to show that human beings can maintain good government from reflection and choice. This, after all, is the ultimate question from the modern period. No gods, angels, kings, or special classes are supposed to govern this country; the "people" are. Surely history since the birth of the United States has underscored the frailty of human beings, and, since people are flawed, good rule by them is always questionable. In that sense, Hamilton's charge remains operative. We must continue to show that we are capable of good government in order to justify the Constitution. Alternately, the Constitution is likewise justified if it provides the tools to maintain good government even in the face of occasional bad governors. Finally, the question invariably intrudes as to whether the Constitution's tools are adequate for the severe challenges of the late twentieth century.

Both its secular nature and its antiquity would seem to mark the Constitution for careful scrutiny as the country enters its third century. Such scrutiny was one central aim of the Douglass Adair Symposia, a series of seven meetings that transpired during the winter and spring of 1986. Named for the late professor of history at the Claremont Graduate School and longtime influential editor of the *William and Mary Quarterly,* the symposia brought together a variety of thoughtful and stimulating perspectives on the country's fundamental document.

Herein are contained the presentations and commentaries from the symposia. The participants included in this anthology do not all come from the same academic or professional background; they are historians, political scientists, lawyers, judges, activists, and essayists, an eclectic array who themselves exhibit the exemplary characteristics of civic virtue that would have pleased the Founders. Thus, the kind of coherence that might be expected, for example, from only historians does not obtain in this work. Nonetheless, the wide variety of perspectives proved of considerable interest to the large audiences attracted to the symposia and fulfilled the planners' aim of broadening and enriching the discourse about our country's origin and prospects.

The first essay is contributed by historian LEONARD LEVY, who says that the Declaration of Independence and the Constitution are among "the most important, creative, and dynamic achievements in history." The Declaration, he continues, was the origin and the Constitution the culmination of a comprehensive nationalist and democratic sentiment. Thus, the Constitution and not the Articles of Confederation embodied the "Spirit of '76." Rather than a mere "bundle of compromises," it reflected a consensus about the fundamental characteristics of a national government. In marked opposition to the followers of Charles Beard, Levy argues that the Constitution coupled nationalism with "mitigated democracy" rather than with antimajoritarianism.

JOYCE APPLEBY agrees in general with Professor Levy. However, she offers several important qualifications to his thesis: first, that nationalism is only compatible with democracy if government is used to promote economic democracy; second, that our freedom is due essentially to the weakness of our government—we are the beneficiaries of nationalism and "unintended" democracy; third, the Constitution provides the means to popular power and personal rights, but these rights must be secured continuously by living men and women; and finally, it would serve us well in this period of self-congratulatory celebration to note the skepticism of Thomas Jefferson and to temper our reverence for the Constitution with an eye to change, when necessary.

Full and equal participation in the American polity seems both a promise of the Declaration and the meaning of modern democracy. RICHARD MORRIS contrasts the theory of equality embodied in the Declaration with the practice of inequality implicit in the original Constitution, wherein, he notes, the word "equality" does not appear. He reminds us that the forgotten people of the Constitution were blacks, women, debtors, indentured servants, and Native Americans. His scholarship makes a valuable contribution to a deeper understanding of how the notion of democratic participation has evolved over two hundred years.

YOLANDA MOSES agrees with Morris by examining the fallacy of the Beard thesis and by offering an impressive list of expanded rights and practices of participation. She underscores the evolution of the Constitution to include in the political process the very people Morris noted were originally left out.

The Founders, like most eighteenth-century thinkers, believed that a republic required on the part of its citizens civic virtue, that is, a loving commitment to the common purpose. Montesquieu had insisted that such virtue could be found only in a small republic where there was a homogeneity of views and people. Yet ours was to be a large, heterogeneous country. Could we find the requisite virtue to assure the continuance of the Republic, or would we degenerate into squabbling special interests, insensitive to the common good and thus incapable of governing for the interest of the whole? The Founders thought long and hard about this, and the issue certainly has relevance in the late twentieth century. SARAH WEDDINGTON defines civic virtue as active public-spiritedness. By relating her personal experiences as a lawyer who practiced before the Supreme Court and as an assistant to President Jimmy Carter, she makes a persuasive case for more women in leadership roles and the need for ways to train more citizens for civic activity. In an age of increased self-interest and private purposes, Weddington reminds us that civic virtue and public leadership have a price.

JUDGE CHARLES WIGGINS, a former mayor and member of Congress, notes that Ms. Weddington's own life of civic virtue has been made possible in part by an evolving democratic system. As do several of the symposia's participants, Wiggins points out the crucial importance of the Civil War and the constitutional amendments that followed. Unlike many of his symposia colleagues, however, he singles out the Electoral College as perhaps the last constitutional impediment to complete popular participation.

Next to voting, party membership is the most common form of political participation. AUSTIN RANNEY describes the antiparty bias of the Constitution and then succinctly traces the roots and growth of political parties in the United States. Taking note of the unique brilliance of James Madison's *The Federalist* No. 10, Ranney explains the Founders' fear of faction. He believes, as does Joyce Appleby, that the Founders' intent was not to create a government that would do good things but rather a government that would be kept from doing bad things. In order for government to do good things, he says, political parties were and are inevitable and necessary—the twin engines of our large-scale democracy.

DANIEL MAZMANIAN is in basic agreement with Ranney's description of the history and necessity of political parties, but he is not sanguine about their future. He believes that the last two decades have seen a rapid and profound diminution of the traditional role and function of parties. The cause, he contends, has been a reemergence of the worst-case scenario described by Madison in *The Federalist* No. 10. No longer are parties grand coalitions but mere vehicles for a political process driven by factionalized, acrimonious, self-seeking, and self-righteous motives. With Ranney, he muses on ways we might act to revitalize the party system.

Addressing what is perhaps the quintessential act of democratic participation—voting—LANI GUINIER's primary concern is with the establishment of full political participation for blacks and other minorities. Contending that in some parts of the United States there is a "crippling lack of enforcement" of voting laws, she traces the political and judicial history of voting rights in this country. Guinier points out that voting is but the first step toward full political participation and urges government to take complete responsibility for universal suffrage.

In near perfect harmony with Guinier's concerns, JUSTICE STANLEY MOSK adds a detailed analysis of many judicial decisions involving voting and elections. Noting that rational voting is an important goal, he describes several factors that contribute to irrational voting practices. Mosk then examines carefully the pros and cons of multilingual and all-English ballots, and he raises troubling questions about the techniques of "direct democracy" (the initiative, referendum, and recall) which surfaced in several states in the early twentieth century.

In the place of a formal essay, the contribution by WILLIAM F. BUCKLEY, JR., is a wide-ranging interview. Describing the Constitution as "the most pliable instrument since Silly Putty," Buckley, in his familiar but no less shocking way, takes issue with many of the nostrums of popular democracy. Foremost is his belief that there is little or no correlation between an increase in democratic participation and the positive quality or character of government. In fact, he argues, the primary contribution of an ever expanding franchise has been an equal expansion of governmental largesse. While agreeing with the need for some system of codified laws and limitations, Buckley questions the role of the Supreme Court as the final arbiter of morality.

HARRY JAFFA has written perhaps the most political and timely of all the symposia essays. He challenges the arguments of Attorney General Edwin Meese regarding the Founders' "original intent" by offering a provocative insight into the relationship between the Declaration and the Constitution. In a clear contradiction of the attorney general, Jaffa contends that the Constitution, prior to the Civil War and the amendments that followed it, was not against or even neutral toward slavery. The intent of the Constitution and its framers, he argues, was proslavery. He supports his position with historical evidence and a subtle examination of the epistemology of the founding documents, maintaining that we and Meese must look to the Declaration and not the Constitution to learn the original intent of the Founders.

Summing up those themes invariably at the base of his scholarly labors, JAMES MACGREGOR BURNS stresses that the constitutional system has serious flaws and deficiencies in light of the enormous anticipated pressures of the next one hundred to two hundred years. The keys to these flaws, he explains, are the breakdown of an effective and responsible two-party system and the emergence of an imperial presidency caused by the need to respond to crises. He recommends a series of constitutional reforms, which he believes will help us to meet the unknown and unknowable crises of the future.

ROBERT DAWIDOFF suggests some reasons why Professor Burns's desire for structural change might not be in our best interest. Basing his analysis on what can be called an aesthetic appreciation of the Constitution as it stands, Dawidoff praises the document's obstructionist characteristics: its ability to "delay rather than deny." The purpose of the Constitution, he notes, is to make more effective the exaggerated promise of the Declaration. For him, the Constitution is a fair reflection of reality; it offers us a serious view of the human condition, a condition marked by the fact that humans are not angels. Coming full circle to the initial point made by his colleague Professor Levy, Dawidoff tells us that "you can really live a life trying to figure out Jefferson's hard mystery, wandering in Madison's curious maze."

As the presentations of this anthology indicate, the issues of governance are as prominent today as they were in the eighteenth century. Moreover, while certain matters regarding politics—a quintessential human pursuit—cannot simply be resolved at any point in history, the issues underscored in this collection should aid us in our deliberations about the meaning and validity of the American experiment. The inherent theme connecting all the essays is the history and future of democratic participation under the Constitution. We have witnessed in the last two hundred years an incredible expansion of the right to participate in the political system, thereby fulfilling the apparent promise of our Revolutionary rhetoric. Serious questions remain, however, as noted throughout the Douglass Adair Symposia. Why, if the political process is so open and accessible, is there such apathy and cynicism among the electorate? Has opening politics to everyone resulted in good government? What about the darkly hinted prognoses of early critics like Alexis de Tocqueville and Henry Adams that committing our nation to both individual liberty and mass democracy would result in mediocre government, uncreative culture, and sullen selfishness?

Civic virtue, as Sarah Weddington has pointed out, is the means by which thoughtful Americans now, as well as two hundred years ago, believe we can overcome the inevitable attendant ills of mass government. Civic virtue is intended to refine individual passion and interest, majority-powered conformity, and potential tyranny into selfless action for the common good. How, then, does the Constitution guarantee this desired refinement? Madison might say that the Constitution ensures this through the ameliorative effects of institutions, particularly institutions that balance and check one another, thereby making it possible but not easy to act. When action is taken, there is a consensus among several groups about the action rather than agreement only among a like-minded majority faction.

To assure this balanced system, Madison, along with Hamilton, foresaw a nation diverse in its interests, religious sects, and kinds of people. Contrary to virtually all the prevailing opinions of their time, the Founders believed such multiplicity was the necessary ingredient to maintain republicanism in a geographically large country. The Declaration was to be the inspiration, the Constitution the rule book, *The Federalist* the philosophy, and a diverse commercial economy the environment for this novel enterprise. But the Founders shared with the thinkers of their time, as we apparently share with them, the conviction that a republic can be sustained only if its people are virtuous, act with commitment and concern for the public interest, and are capable of reflecting on their condition as well as of making choices to assure a better future. This is the injunction Hamilton proffered in *The Federalist* No. 1. It is the challenge taken up by the Douglass Adair Symposia. In fact, Professor Adair would instruct us to share the Founders' insistence, remembering that a democratic republic is a grand yet fragile experiment, demanding the best of every citizen.

John Allphin Moore, Jr.
John E. Murphy

Contributors

DAVID L. LEVERING is a professor of history at California State Polytechnic University, Pomona. He served as chair of the California Commission on Teacher Credentialing from 1982 to 1984.

JOHN ALLPHIN MOORE, JR., director of the Douglass Adair Symposia, is professor of American studies at California State Polytechnic University, Pomona, and coauthor with Myron Roberts of *The Pursuit of Happiness: Government and Politics in America.*

JOHN E. MURPHY is a consultant to the Douglass Adair Symposia. He has been a teacher for the California Youth Authority since 1972.

LEONARD W. LEVY, Andrew W. Mellon All-Claremont Professor of Humanities at the Claremont Colleges, has written extensively on the Constitution and the Bill of Rights. His book on the origins of the Fifth Amendment won the Pulitzer Prize in 1969, and he is editor of the four-volume *Encyclopedia of the American Constitution.*

JOYCE APPLEBY, a former student of Douglass Adair, is professor of history at the University of California, Los Angeles. Her latest book is *Capitalism and a New Social Order: The Republican Vision of the 1970's.*

RICHARD B. MORRIS is Gouverneur Morris Professor Emeritus of History at Columbia University, a former president of the American Historical Association, editor of the John Jay Papers, and cochair of Project '87. He is also the author of numerous respected works on the Revolutionary and founding periods of American history.

YOLANDA T. MOSES is a professor of anthropology and dean of the School of Arts, California State Polytechnic University, Pomona.

SARAH WEDDINGTON is a law professor, magazine columnist, political commentator, former Texas state legislator, and attorney who has argued successfully before the U.S. Supreme Court. As a chief assistant to President Jimmy Carter, she was responsible for issues affecting women and minority communities.

JUDGE CHARLES E. WIGGINS has served as mayor of El Monte, California, a member of the U.S. Congress, and currently sits on the Federal Court of Appeals. He also serves as a presidential appointee to the Constitution's Bicentennial Commission.

AUSTIN RANNEY, a former president of the American Political Science Association and resident senior scholar at the American Enterprise Institute for Public Policy Research, is professor of political science at the University of California, Berkeley. He is well known for his many publications on American elections, political parties, and the impact of television on politics.

DANIEL A. MAZMANIAN is director of the Center for Politics and Policy and Luther Lee Professor of Government at the Claremont Graduate School. His most recent book is *Implementing Public Policy*.

C. LANI GUINIER, of the NAACP Legal Defense and Educational Fund, is a graduate of Yale Law School, a former special assistant to the Civil Rights Division of the U.S. Department of Justice, and an adjunct professor at New York University Law School. She has been closely involved in key voting rights cases throughout the country.

JUSTICE STANLEY MOSK has had a distinguished tenure on the Supreme Court of California, before which he served as the state's attorney general.

WILLIAM F. BUCKLEY, JR., is one of the most visible political thinkers in the United States. Founder of the *National Review,* host of PBS's "Firing Line," and author of numerous essays and books, he has been the dominant influence in post-World War II conservative thought.

HARRY V. JAFFA, who has written seminal works on Aristotelian political thought, the Declaration of Independence, and the Constitution, as well as on the Lincoln-Douglas debates, is Henry Salvatori Professor of Political Philosophy at Claremont McKenna College.

JAMES MACGREGOR BURNS is Woodrow Wilson Professor of Political Science at Williams College, a former president of the American Political Science Association, cochair of Project '87, and author of prize-winning books on Franklin Roosevelt, presidential leadership, and the Constitution. He is currently completing a trilogy on American political and intellectual history.

ROBERT DAWIDOFF, author of a critically acclaimed biography of John Randolph, writes extensively in both scholarly and popular publications. He is professor of history at the Claremont Graduate School.

The Making of the Constitution, 1776–1789

Leonard W. Levy

On July 4, 1776, King George III wrote in his diary: "Nothing of importance this day." When the news of the Declaration of Independence reached him, he still could not know how wrong he had been. The political philosophy of social compact, natural rights, and limited government—the philosophy that generated the Declaration of Independence—also spurred the most important, creative, and dynamic constitutional achievements in history; the Declaration itself was only the beginning. Within a mere thirteen years, Americans invented or first institutionalized a Bill of Rights against all branches of government, the written Constitution, the Constitutional Convention, Federalism, judicial review, and a solution to the colonial problem (admitting territories to the Union as states fully equal to the original thirteen). Religious liberty, separation of church and state, political parties, separation of powers, an acceptance of the principle of equality, and the conscious creation of a new nation were also among American institutional "firsts," although not all these initially appeared between 1776 and 1789. In that brief span of time, Americans created what are today the oldest major republic, the oldest political democracy, the oldest state constitution, and the oldest national constitution. These unparalleled achievements derived not from originality in speculative theory but from the constructive application of old ideas, which Americans took so seriously that they constitutionally based their institutions of government on them.

From thirteen separate colonies the Second Continental Congress "brought forth a new nation," as Abraham Lincoln said. When he declared that "the Union is older than the States, and in fact created them as States," Lincoln meant that the Union (Congress) came first and that the Declaration of Independence, which asserted that the colonies had become states, derived from the authority of the "United States."

Contrary to the usual view, the "spirit of '76" tended to be nationalistic, not localistic. The members of Congress represented the states and acted on state instructions, but they also acted for the new nation, and the form of government they thought proper in 1776 was a centralized one. Benjamin Franklin had proposed such a government in July 1775, when he presented to Congress "Articles of Confederation and perpetual Union." He urged a congressional government with an executive committee that would manage "general continental Business and Interests" and a Congress empowered to determine war and peace, make treaties, settle all disputes between the colonies, plant new colonies, and make laws for "the general Welfare" concerning matters on which individual colonies "cannot be competent," such as "our general Commerce" and "general Currency." Franklin's plan of union was too radical in July 1775, when independence remained one year away and reconciliation with Britain on American terms was the object of the war.

As the war continued in 1776, however, nationalist sentiment strengthened. Thomas Paine's *Common Sense* called for American independence and "a Continental form of Government." Nationalism and centralism were twin causes. John Langdon of New Hampshire favored independence and "an American Constitution" that provided for a national congress empowered to govern "in everything of moment relative to governmental matters." Proposals for a centralized union became common by the spring of 1776, and these proposals tended to show democratic impulses. Contrary to conventional views, nationalism and mitigated democracy, not nationalism and conservatism, were related. For example, a New York newspaper urged the popular election of a national congress with a "superintending power" over the individual colonies as to "all commercial and Continental affairs," leaving to each colony control over merely its "internal policy." A Populist plan in a Connecticut newspaper recommended that the congress be empowered to govern "all matters of general concernment" and "every other thing proper and necessary" for the benefit of the whole. The "Spartacus" essays, which newspapers in various colonies printed, disparaged the states or "cantons" with their own legislatures, all united in a national congress with powers similar to those enumerated by Franklin, including a paramount power to "interfere" with a colony's local affairs whenever required by "the good of the continent." "Essex" reminded his readers that "the strength and happiness of America must be Continental, not Provincial, and that whatever appears to be for the good of the whole must be submitted to by every Part." He advocated dividing the colonies into many smaller equal parts that would have equal representation in a powerful national congress chosen directly by the people, including taxpaying widows.

Given the prevalence of such views in the first half of 1776, a representative committee of the Continental Congress probably mirrored public opinion when it framed a nationalist plan for confederation. On July 12 a thirteen-member committee chaired by John Dickinson of Pennsylvania presented to Congress a plan that borrowed heavily from Franklin's. The Committee of the Whole of Congress adopted the Dickinson draft with few changes.

The plan was similar to Franklin's, except that Congress had no power over "general commerce." But Congress, acting for the United States, was clearly paramount to the individual states, which were not even referred to as "states." Collectively, they were "the United States of America"; otherwise, they were styled "colonies" or "colony," terms not compatible with state sovereignty, to which no reference was made. Indeed, the draft merely reserved to each colony control "of its internal policy, in all matters that shall not interfere with the Articles of this Confederation." That crucial provision made even "internal policy" subordinate to congressional powers and highlighted the nationalist character of the proposed confederation.

The Dickinson draft of the Articles reported by the Committee of the Whole provoked dissension in Congress. Because of disagreements and the urgency of prosecuting the war, Congress failed to settle on a plan of union in 1776. By the spring of 1777 the nationalist momentum was spent. By then most of the states had adopted constitutions and had legitimate governments.

Previously, provisional governments had controlled the states, and they had looked to the Continental Congress for leadership and approval, but the creation of legitimate state governments reinvigorated old provincial loyalties. Politicians, whose careers were locally oriented, feared a strong central government as a rival institution. By April 1777, when state sovereignty triumphed, only seventeen of the forty-eight congressmen who had been members of the Committee of the Whole that adopted the Dickinson draft remained in Congress. Most of the new congressmen opposed centralized government. They killed the key nationalist clause and replaced it with this substitute provision, which then became part of the Articles as finally adopted: "Each State retains its sovereignty, freedom and independence, and every power, jurisdiction and right, which is not by this confederation expressly delegated to the United States in Congress assembled." That motion carried, sapping the powers of the national government.

In the autumn of 1777 a Congress dominated by state-sovereignty advocates completed the plan of confederation. Nationalists, who favored proportionate representation in Congress with every delegate entitled to vote, lost badly to those who favored voting by states with each state having one vote. Thereafter, the populous wealthy states had no interest in supporting a strong national government that could be controlled by the votes of lesser states.

After the nationalist spurt of 1776 proved insufficient to produce the Articles, the states crippled the Confederation. Even as colonies the states had been particularistic, jealous, and uncooperative. Centrifugal forces originating in diversity—of economics, geography, religion, class structure, and race—produced sectional, provincial, and local loyalties that could not be overcome during a war against the centralized powers claimed by Parliament. The controversy with Britain had produced passions and principles that made the Franklin and Dickinson drafts unviable. Not even those nationalist drafts empowered Congress to tax, although the principle of no taxation without representation had become irrelevant as to Congress, a representative body. Similarly, Congress as late as 1774 had acknowledged Parliament's legitimate "regulation of our external commerce," but in 1776 Congress denied that Parliament had any authority over America, and by 1777 Americans were unwilling to grant their own central legislature powers they preferred their provincial assemblies to wield. Above all, most states refused to put their trust in any central authority that a few large states might dominate, absent a constitutionally based principle of state equality. Accordingly, the Articles of Confederation, ratified in 1781, failed to embody the democratic and nationalistic impulses of 1776. Contrary to Charles Beard and Merrill Jensen, the Constitution of 1787, not the Articles of 1781, embodied the spirit of '76.

The Constitution of 1787 was impossible in 1781, or at any time before it was framed. The Articles were an indispensable transitional stage in the development of the Constitution. Not even the Constitution would have been ratified in 1789 if the Framers had submitted it for approval to the state legislatures that kept Congress paralyzed in the 1780s. Congress possessed expressly delegated powers with no means of enforcing them. That Congress lacked commerce and tax powers was a serious deficiency, but not nearly so crippling as its lack of sanctions and the failure of the states to abide by the Articles. Congress simply could not make anyone, except soldiers, do anything; it acted on the states and not on people. Only a national government that could execute its laws independently of the states could have survived.

The states flouted their constitutional obligations. The Articles obliged the states to "abide by the determinations of the United States, in Congress assembled," but there was no way to make them comply. The states were not sovereign except as to their internal police and tax powers; rather, they behaved unconstitutionally, and there was no remedy for that.

One of the extraordinary achievements of the Articles was the creation of a rudimentary federal system. It failed because its central government did not operate directly on individuals within its sphere of authority. The Confederation had no independent executive and judicial branches because the need for them scarcely existed when Congress addressed its acts mainly to the states. The framers of the Articles distributed the powers of government with remarkable acumen, committing to Congress about all that belonged to a central government except taxation and commercial regulation, the two powers that Americans of the Revolutionary War believed to be part of state sovereignty. Even Alexander Hamilton, who in 1780 advocated that Congress should have "complete sovereignty," approved of "raising money by internal taxes."

The controversy with Britain had taught that liberty and localism were congruent. The 1780s taught that excessive localism was incompatible with nationhood. The Confederation was a necessary point of midpassage. It bequeathed to the United States the fundamentals of a federal system, a national domain, the Northwest Ordinance—a solution to the colonial problem—and a working government bureaucracy. Otherwise, the United States was a failure.

By contrast, state government flourished. Except for Rhode Island and Connecticut, all the states adopted written constitutions during the war, eight in 1776. The Virginia constitution of 1776, the first permanent state constitution, began with a Declaration of Rights, the first in history to restrain all branches of government. All state constitutions prior to the Massachusetts constitution of 1780 were framed by legislatures, no matter what they called themselves. Massachusetts originated a new institution of government, a specially elected constitutional convention whose sole function was to frame a constitution and submit it for popular ratification. That procedure became the standard, and Massachusetts's constitution, which is still operative, became the model American state constitution. Massachusetts also was the first state to give more than lip service to the principle of separation of powers. (Elsewhere, unbalanced government and legislative supremacy prevailed.) It established the precedent for a strong, popularly elected executive with a veto power, the model for the American presidency. And judicial review originated at the state level before the Philadelphia Constitutional Convention of 1787.

By 1787 even men who had defended state sovereignty conceded the necessity of a national convention. William Grayson of Virginia admitted that "the present Confederation is utterly inefficient and that if it remains much longer in its present State of imbecility we shall be one of the most contemptible Nations on the face of the earth." Luther Martin of Maryland admitted that Congress was "weak, contemptibly weak," and Richard Henry Lee believed that no government "short of force, will answer." "Do you not think," he asked George Mason, "that it ought to be declared...that any State act of legislation that shall contravene, or oppose, the authorized acts of Congress shall be ipso facto void, and of no force whatsoever?" Many leaders, like Thomas Jefferson, advocated executive and judicial branches for the national government and appeals from state courts to a federal court "in all cases where the act of Confederation controlled the question." A consensus was developing.

The Constitutional Convention, which began on May 25, 1787, lasted almost four months yet reached its most crucial decisions almost at the outset. The first order of business was the nationalistic Virginia Plan, and the first vote of the Convention, acting as a Committee of the Whole, was the adoption of a resolution "that a national Government ought to be established consisting of a supreme legislative, Executive and Judiciary." Thus, the Convention immediately agreed on abandoning, rather than amending, the Articles; on writing a new Constitution; on creating a national government that would be supreme; and on having it consist of three branches.

The radical character of this early decision may be best understood by comparing it with the Articles. The Articles failed mainly because there was no way to force the states to fulfill their obligations or to obey the exercise of such powers as Congress did possess. The vice of the existing Confederation, said Hamilton, "is the principle of legislation for states or governments, in their corporate capacities, as contradistinguished from the individuals of which they consist." At once, the convention remedied that vital defect in the Articles, as Mason approvingly observed, by agreeing on a government that "could directly operate on individuals." Thus, the Framers solved the critical problem of sanctions by establishing a national government independent of the states.

On the third day of business the Committee of the Whole made other crucial decisions, with little or no debate. One, reflecting the nationalist bias of the Convention, established a bicameral system whose larger house was to be elected directly by the people rather than by the state legislatures. Mason, no less, explained: "Under the existing confederacy, Congress represents the States, not the people of the States; their acts operate on the States, not on the individuals. The case will be changed in the new plan of Government. The people will be represented, they ought therefore to choose the Representatives." Another early decision vested in the Congress the sweeping and undefined power, recommended by the Virginia Plan, "to legislate in all cases to which the separate States are incompetent; or in which the harmony of the U.S. may be interrupted by the exercise of individual [state] legislation; to negative all laws passed by the several States contravening in the opinion of the National Legislature the articles of Union, or any treaties subsisting under the authority of the Union." Not one state voted "nay" to this exceptionally nationalistic proposition nor opposed the decision of the next day to create a national executive with broad, undefined powers.

However, some delegates were alarmed, not because of an excessive centralization of powers in the national government but because of the advantages given to the largest states at the expense of the others. Three states—Virginia, Massachusetts, and Pennsylvania—had 45 percent of the white population in the country. Under the proposed scheme of proportionate representation, the small states feared that the large ones would dominate the others by controlling the national government.

The Paterson, or New Jersey, Plan was a small-states plan, not a states'-rights one; it, too, had a strong nationalist orientation. It retained state equality in Congress, but it vested in Congress one of the two critical powers previously lacking: "to pass Acts for the regulation of trade and commerce," foreign and interstate. The other, the power of taxation, appeared only in a stunted form. Otherwise, the Paterson Plan proposed the same powers for the national legislature as the finished Constitution. The plan also contained the basis of the national supremacy clause of the Constitution.

After debating the two plans—Virginia and New Jersey—the Committee of the Whole voted in favor of the original recommendations based on the Virginia Plan. Thus, after only three weeks, the

Framers decisively agreed, for the second time, on a strong independent national government that would operate directly on individuals without the involvement of states.

The objections of the small states were satisfied by the Great Compromise: proportionate representation in the lower house and state equality in the Senate. The compromise saved small-state prestige and the Convention from failure. Thereafter, consensus on fundamentals was restored, with the small-state delegates becoming fervent supporters of centralism. For example, there was a motion that each state should be represented by two senators who would "vote per capita," that is, as individuals. Martin protested that per capita voting conflicted with the very idea of "the States being represented," yet the motion carried 9 to 1, with no further debate.

On many matters of structure, mechanics, and detail there were angry disagreements, but agreement prevailed on the essentials. The office of the presidency is a good illustration. That there should be a powerful chief executive provoked no great debate, but the Convention almost broke up on the method of electing him. Some matters of detail, however, occasioned practically no disagreement and revealed the nationalist consensus. Mason, of all people, moved that one qualification of congressmen should be "citizenship of the United States," and no one disagreed. Under the Articles of Confederation, there was only state citizenship; that there should be a concept of national citizenship seemed natural to men framing a constitution for a nation. Even more a revelation of the nationalist consensus was that three of the most crucial provisions of the Constitution—the taxing power, the necessary-and-proper clause, and the supremacy clause—were accepted casually and unanimously, without debate.

Until midway during its sessions, the Convention did not take the trouble to define with care the distribution of power between the national government and the states, although the very nature of the "federal" system depended on that distribution. Consensus on fundamentals once again provides the explanation. Significantly, the first enumerated power was that of taxation and the second that of regulating commerce among the states and with foreign nations: the two principal powers withheld from Congress by the Articles. When the Convention voted on the provision that Congress "shall have the power to lay and collect taxes, duties, imposts and excises," the states were unanimous and only one delegate was opposed. When the Convention next turned to the commerce power, there was no discussion and everyone voted affirmatively.

Notwithstanding its enumeration of the legislative powers, all of which the Convention accepted, the Committee on Detail added an omnibus clause that has served as an ever expanding source of national authority: "And to make all laws that shall be necessary and proper for carrying into execution the foregoing powers." The Convention agreed to that clause without a single dissenting vote by any state or delegate. The history of the great supremacy clause, Article VI, shows a similar consensus: this Constitution, all laws made in pursuance thereof, and all U.S. treaties shall be "the supreme law of the land." Without debate the Convention adopted the supremacy clause, and not one state or delegate voted "nay."

Why was there such a consensus? The obvious answer, apart from the fact that opponents either stayed away or walked out, is that experience had proved to the American people that the nationalist constitutional position was right. If the United States was to survive and flourish, a strong national government had to be established. The Framers were accountable to public opinion; the Convention was a representative body. That its members were prosperous, well-educated political leaders made them no less representative than the Congress of the Confederation. The state legislatures, which elected Congress, also elected the nationalist members of the Convention. The state legislatures could not thwart the popular will, nor could the Framers. They could not do as they pleased, and they were not free to promulgate the Constitution. Although they adroitly arranged for its ratification by nine state ratifying conventions rather than by all state legislatures, they could not present a plan that the people of the states would not tolerate. They could not control the membership of those state ratifying conventions. They could not even be sure that the existing Congress would submit the Constitution to the states for ratification, let alone for ratification by state conventions that had to be specially elected. If the Framers strayed too far from public opinion, their work would have been wasted. The consensus in the Convention coincided with an emerging consensus in the country that recaptured the nationalist spirit of '76. That the Union had to be strengthened was an almost universal American belief.

For its time the Constitution was a remarkably democratic document framed by democratic methods. The Convention elected by the state legislatures and consisting of many of the foremost leaders of their time deliberated for almost four months. Its members included many opponents of the finished scheme, and sixteen of the fifty-five members did not sign it. The nation knew the Convention was considering changes in the government. When the proposed Constitution was made public, voters in every state were asked to choose delegates to vote for or against it after open debate. The use of state ratifying conventions fit the theory that a new fundamental law was being adopted and, therefore, conventions were proper for the task. Thus, the Congress of the Confederation submitted the Constitution to the states, calling for the election of the ratifying conventions.

The Constitution guaranteed to each state a republican or representative form of government and fixed no property or religious qualifications on the right to vote or hold office, during a period when such qualifications were common. By leaving voting qualifications to the states, the Constitution implicitly accepted such qualifications but imposed none. Unlike the Articles, the Constitution created a Congress whose lower house was popularly elected. When only three states directly elected their chief executive officer, the Constitution provided for the election of the president by an Electoral College that originated in the people and is still operative. The Constitution's system of separation of powers and elaborate checks and balances was not intended to refine out popular influence on government but to protect liberty; the Framers divided, distributed, and limited powers to prevent any branch, faction, interest, or section from becoming too powerful. Checks and balances were not undemocratic, and the Framers were hard-pressed to convince opponents, who wanted far more checks and balances, that the Constitution had enough. Although the Framers were not democrats in the modern sense, their opponents were even less democratic. Those opponents sought to capitalize on the lack of a Bill of Rights; ratification of the Constitution became possible only because some leading Federalists committed themselves to amendments as soon as the new government went into operation. When that happened, Anti-Federalists opposed a Bill of Rights because it would allay popular fears of the new government, thus ending the chance for state sovereignty amendments.

The Constitution is basically a political document. Modern scholarship has completely discredited the once popular view, associated with Charles Beard, that the Constitution was made undemocratically to advance the economic interests of personal property groups, chiefly creditors. In conclusion, the Constitution was framed and ratified because most voters came to understand that a strong central government was indispensable for nationhood.

Commentary to Leonard Levy

Joyce Appleby

Leonard Levy has presented a consensus view of the Constitution. He has made three principal points, all of them against popular wisdom. Contrary to the usual view, he has said that the "spirit of '76" tended to be nationalistic, not localistic, and that nationalism and mitigated democracy, not nationalism and conservatism, were related. Finally, contrary to Charles Beard, who for many years countered the popular view, Levy has contended that the Constitution of 1787, not the Articles of 1781, embodied the spirit of '76.

Looking more closely at these propositions, I will first examine the relationship of the Articles of Confederation and the spirit of '76 and make a stronger case than was made earlier for the contribution of that period. It might be better for us to say *spirits* of '76 because the acrimonious and passionate ideological debates that broke out in the 1790s destroyed the notion that there was a single spirit of '76, a single set of problems and solutions, or a single interpretation of the significance of the American Revolution. Indeed, there was a great deal of debate as to whether or not it had been a revolution or whether it should simply be called a war for independence.

Levy has dealt with the contribution of the period of the Articles, describing that time as an indispensable transition, but he has laid his stress upon the fact that the initial nationalistic spirit of 1776 gave way to a period of state sovereignty and the assertion of state supremacy in 1777, with the Articles that then were drafted. I am certainly not in disagreement with that. But there is a story behind the drafting of the Articles of Confederation that is worth retelling and bears on the point of both nationalism and democracy. The Articles, drafted in 1777, were not ratified until 1781. What was going on during this four-year period? Of course, a war was being fought, but more importantly, one state—Maryland—dug in its heels and refused to sign the Articles until those states (of which Maryland was not one) like Virginia, Massachusetts, South Carolina, North

11

Carolina, Connecticut, and New York gave up their sea-to-sea land claims. It was Maryland's point that the unoccupied land to the west, however far it might go (since they did not know then exactly where the Pacific Ocean was), would accrue to the states only through a successful war for independence. Therefore, since it was a national war, the states should give up their claim to distant land. This was a reasonable position, although, needless to say, the states with the claims did not wish to concede.

This was not all of the story. Thomas Jefferson realized, as did others, that behind Maryland's wish to have this land ceded by the states were large land companies with claims to the unoccupied land in the West. What happened? In good American political fashion, a compromise was worked out: Jefferson and others saw to it that Virginia, which had by far the largest claim, would cede its land to the Continental Congress—to the nation, as it were—if all other claims to the land were extinguished. In other words, neither the states nor the land companies would have any prior claim, and the land indeed would become a national domain to be won by the states in a successful war. This, I think, was an extraordinarily important act, both in terms of democracy and nationalism, and it was followed by the Northwest Ordinance, also passed by the Continental Congress. The Northwest Ordinance is famous for many reasons, but certainly one of its major triumphs was its provision for the orderly admission of new states on a parity with the old states. In both of these acts, therefore, we find the Continental Congress making a major contribution to nationalism and democracy—so much of a contribution that I even would want to add to the thirty-nine signers of the Constitution a fortieth Founding Father in Jefferson. Nationalism is only compatible with democracy if government is used to facilitate economic democracy. And this is what happened with the creation of a national domain and, subsequently, with the land policies which Jefferson as president put into effect.

Professor Levy's second proposition is the idea that nationalism and a mitigated democracy go together. Again, I would agree with him but would change the adjective to say that nationalism and *unintended* or *incidental* democracy went together in 1787. The large states that championed democracy—that is, championed proportional voting for the legislature—did so in large part because numbers were on their side. As large states, they would benefit from having proportional representatives in both houses of the legislature. This did not mean that ordinary voters would not secure something by this. Proportional representation, as it came out in the lower house, did mean that ordinary voters, or all voters, had more representation in the federal government under the Constitution than they had under the Articles of Confederation. But the contribution to democracy, the actual direct contribution to democracy of the large states, is much less clear. It seems that the test of democracy and the association of democracy and the large states would lie in the use of power within the states and would be determined by how much democracy existed therein, measured by the distribution of representatives for state legislatures, the ease of voting, and the tendencies of the laws themselves. Here the record of large states in promoting democracy is not so positive. Slavery is a glaring flaw, and Virginia obviously was a slave state, but there were fights over property qualifications for voting, for the reform of municipal corporations, and for redistricting. These were all battles to be fought for democracy.

There was an astounding amount of intrusion of state power in personal lives. By concentrating on the limitations of federal power, we sometimes forget that people lived under a dual sovereignty and that the sovereign states, even under the Constitution, were capable of legislating in areas that, to our mind today, were quite astounding. There was an established church in Massachusetts and in other large states until well into the nineteenth century, and in our own lifetime states have been able to determine what we may legally drink, whom we may legally marry or not marry, to whom we may legally make love, and the limits of the expressions of that love. We deflect the knowledge of these powerful intrusions on our personal freedom.

I wish to emphasize the point that, although Americans have been peculiarly free and that we should celebrate this fact during the Bicentennial, our freedom is not necessarily derived from the institutions in the way that we think it is. I would say, rather, that our freedom can be ascribed to the weakness of our government. That is part of the checks and balances Professor Levy has talked about, ranging from the cultural hostility to authoritarian institutions to the variety of interests James Madison counted on to check majority faction. Such diversity of occupations, religions, and family backgrounds has made us all keenly aware, for example, that the cause of a Jehovah's Witness in refusing to salute the flag is our cause, even if we may not agree with the particular act. The larger point is that the Constitution does not guarantee popular power and personal rights; it provides the means to them. Popular power and personal rights are secured generation after generation by living men and women.

One final comment deals with the Bicentennial itself. Contrary to the popular view and the one we will hear frequently stated, the U.S. Constitution, ratified in 1788 and put into operation in 1789, did not last two hundred years. In fact, it lasted only seventy-two years. In 1861 the Union was rent asunder. The government of the United States resumed control of the compacting states only after a bloody civil war. It even could be argued that the Constitution not only did not inhibit the conflicts between the states but also exacerbated them. More to the point, the Civil War broke out for the very reasons that the Continental Congress, under the Articles of Confederation, was flawed. As Professor Levy has reminded us, the Continental Congress simply could not make anyone, except soldiers, do anything. Congress acted on the states and not on people. And more prophetically, Levy has told us, only a national government able to execute its laws independently of the states could have survived. On issues relating to slavery and to antislavery agitation, on issues like the free circulation of the U.S. mail, Congress and the president faced states, not individuals, and they drew back from enforcement.

Why do I advert to these dreary and well-known facts? To emphasize one spirit of '76, that of my fortieth Founding Father, Jefferson, who ridiculed those who looked at constitutions with sanctimonious reverence and deemed them like the Ark of the Covenant, too sacred to be touched. There is a tendency to celebrate everything about our Constitution. Everything becomes optimal: its openness to diverse interpretations, its lacunae, its impediments to the exercise of legitimate authority. Everything is made to appear normative, both good and typical. We sometimes sound like Edmund Burke, a contemporary of the Founding Fathers, who explained that the English loved their constitution because it had been theirs for time out of mind. This was certainly nobody's spirit of '76. Thus, let us remember what was radical and skeptical and rational in the founding of our institutions and celebrate our capacity to correct, improve, and change our government with the same forcefulness as that of the Founding Fathers.

The People of the Constitution: Persons Remembered and Persons Forgotten

Richard B. Morris

The Constitution proclaims itself to be a creation of "We the People." As the nationalists who drafted it were to interpret the Preamble, that document was adopted by ratifying conventions of the *people of the states* rather than by the states themselves, and its sanctions went directly to the people.[1] Under this new charter of governance, many Americans would enjoy rights and privileges unparalleled in the contemporary world. One could argue that the Constitution reflected that cautiously transforming egalitarianism which marked the Revolutionary era.

The fact is that, unlike the Great Declaration which, as one perceptive scholar has observed, "introduced an egalitarian rhetoric to an unequal society,"[2] the Constitution has no place for the word "equality." The Framers were more concerned about creating an effective national government than in underpinning notions of equality, which they deemed unrealistic if not unattainable. Some of the Founding Fathers were rather emphatic on the subject. "All men are men, and not angels," John Adams observed, "nor are they lions or whales or eagles." In fact, "the most that equality of nature amounts to," he concluded, is that they were "all of the same species."[3] James Madison frequently remarked on the inequality of talents, wealth, and conditions of men, perhaps most notably in *The Federalist* No. 10, while James Wilson told his law students that the declaration that all men are created equal was not meant to apply "to their virtues, their talents, their dispositions, or their acquirements. In all three respects," he added, "there is, and it is fit for the great purposes of society that there should be, great inequality among men."[4]

What the Founding Fathers were committed to was equality of opportunity, an equality made possible by the availability of freehold land under a national land system devised for an expanding frontier.

Equality of opportunity would not be curbed by special privileges, monopolies, titles of nobility, or hereditary honors; rather, it would be promoted in the states by the abolition of primogeniture and entailed estates and by a variety of other reforms in education and in criminal and civil law. The reformers did not aim at social leveling, which the Founding Fathers would have looked on with abhorrence. Still, Madison kept the door ajar. The due process clause in his Bill of Rights would provide a plastic conception, one day to be expanded to include rights which even Madison did not envision. The incorporation principle adopted by the Supreme Court of our century fixed upon the states, as well as upon the federal government, the restraints of a number of the first ten amendments.

The equality that foreign travelers found in America at the time of the adoption of the Constitution was a decline of deference, a trend which fell short of overthrowing the divisions of society by orders or classes. What the American Revolution produced was a sweeping change in the elites: the Patriot Whig elite now supplanting royal officials and affluent Tories. A half century later, Alexis de Tocqueville might fix upon the equality of social condition as "the salient feature of American society," but the destruction of gentry leadership that he was witnessing did not occur in the years of the Confederation.

What observers did find was a cautiously transforming egalitarianism. Political upward mobility was indubitably advanced. In most states, Catholics and Jews were enfranchised and church establishment terminated. Despite the existence of property qualifications for voting—qualifications sidestepped in the Constitution, which leaves such matters to the states—in practice 50 to 80 percent of adult white males were enfranchised, although voter turnouts in these years seldom exceeded 36 percent of adult males. The franchise was not really a serious issue among the working class, which already had substantially won the franchise. What working people were concerned about was their power to control their representatives once they were elected.[5] In so far as holding federal office was concerned, neither the Articles of Confederation nor the Constitution prescribed any property qualifications. Only the Northwest Ordinance set a minimum requirement for its representatives to the territorial assemblies of 210 acres of land in fee simple within the district they represented.

Impressive strides were made during the Confederation years in correcting the inequitable representation of the interior and the up-country, often highlighted by moving state capitals from tidewater to upland. By issuing copious amounts of paper currency, anathema to Madison, or by shifting taxes from polls to property, or from equal acreage to ad valorem taxes, the states in effect were shifting the burdens from the poor to the rich—from the debtor to the creditor—but not universally, or we would not have had Shays' Rebellion concluded only months before the first meeting of the Constitutional Convention.

In no area is the egalitarian impact of the American Revolution era more visible than in the opportunities for new men to enter government as well as business and the professions. The Philadelphia grandee who complained that the Revolution brought all the "dregs" to the top may have had in mind New Jersey's "poor man's lawyer," Abraham Clark; or New York's Abraham Yates, Jr., a shoemaker-lawyer and unreconstructed Anti-Federalist; or the Pennsylvania frontier trio of John Smilie, William Findley, and Robert Whitehill. All bypassed the social hierarchy despite their lack of polish and their meager educational backgrounds. Indeed, socioeconomic mobility of the pre-Revolutionary and Revolutionary years has been a recent focus of significant investigation, and the emergent picture is conflicting, both urban and rural. Clearly the rich were getting richer while the less affluent also were improving their economic prospects, albeit at a decidedly slower pace.[6] However, even the most critical of foreign observers would grudgingly concede that ranks were not fixed as in Europe, while wealth and reputation were fluid and variable.[7]

Certainly the omission of the word "equality" from the Constitution did not deter the working people in the cities and larger towns from giving overwhelming support to the Constitution. Indeed, one of the remarkable stories of the period is the transformation of a radical anti-Tory working class into a fervent supporter of an effective national government that would impose uniform tariffs, prevent foreign dumping, and encourage domestic manufactures. That alliance toward the close of the Confederation period of free labor with business and professional people was evidenced in every leading town where the respective states' ratification of the Constitution was celebrated by great parades, in which participants were arrayed by trades, occupations, and professions. Far from regarding the Constitution as a reaction and betrayal of the American Revolution, as unreconstructed Anti-Federalists viewed it then and Populist-Progressive historians have depicted it in more recent times, the urban workingman hailed it as a fulfillment of the purposes for which the war had been fought: national independence.

That is only a part of the story, however. The original Constitution, we now recognize, was basically a document of governance for free, white, propertied adult males, free from dependence upon others. Left out of its text, or dealt with ambiguously, were the forgotten people—those bound to servitude, white or black (slavery was implicitly, rather than overtly, recognized), debtors, paupers, Indians, and women—most of whom were not considered a part of the political constituency. True, the Founding Fathers held diverse views on the score of blacks, Indians, and women, but they managed to sidestep a direct confrontation on each of these issues. Let us now focus on these forgotten people—in numbers, a majority of the nation's inhabitants in 1787.

I

It may come as a surprise, perhaps, to learn that so many white males fell into the debtor category. These were people who in one form or another were victims of the harsh laws relating to indebtedness. (Perhaps our comprehension of, and sympathy for, the plight of the debtor in the early national era may be quickened when we realize that mortgage foreclosures in the past few years have exceeded any total since the Great Depression years, and that this cyclical problem is still not resolved.) In the 1780s, as Shays' Rebellion highlights, the burden of debt in the wake of the first depression in our history—one beginning in 1784 and continuing down through the establishment of the national government—spared neither poor nor rich. Victims of the speculative orgies of the 1790s, like Robert Morris, William Duer, and even Supreme Court Associate Justice James Wilson, attest to the unrelenting pressures against delinquent debtors.

The men who drafted the Constitution, men of the stamp of Madison, Alexander Hamilton, Gouverneur Morris, and Rufus King, were determined that debtor relief in the form of paper money issued by the states and various forms of moratory legislation should not be tolerated. In *The Federalist* No. 10, Madison expressed his satisfaction that under the Constitution "a rage for paper money, for an abolition of debts, for an equal distribution of property, or for any other improper or wicked project, will be less apt to pervade the whole body of the Union than a particular member of it." The Constitution also reflected Madisonian thinking. It forbade states to issue bills of credit, "make anything but gold or silver coin tender in payment of debts," or enact laws "impairing the obligation of contracts."

Despite the passage of a considerable body of remedial legislation providing partial release from imprisonment for debt, reform of the debt laws in the early national era had a low priority, but there always had been an alternative. Because of the continuing labor shortage, laws enacted in colonial days releasing the debtor from prison to serve his creditor or assigns for a period of time sufficient to discharge the debt remained on the books during the Confederation years, with Massachusetts having the dubious honor of lodging in jail the most highly publicized number of insolvent debtors or selling them off as servants.

A variety of organizations for the relief of insolvent debtors lobbied for a reform of this system, but at best only partial relief was provided by the states on the eve of the convention. In fact, if there was a reform movement against incarceration of defaulting debtors, it clearly was directed toward the merchant and the speculator, not the workingman and the small farmer. Such discrimination was frankly avowed by Zephaniah Swift, the Connecticut jurist writing at the close of the century. Swift differentiated between the honest and the fraudulent debtor as regards treatment at law, while making a further distinction between laboring men and persons of substantial property, a distinction that few would be willing to accept as valid in our own time.[8] In sum, at the time of the adoption of the Constitution, the elimination of servitude for white debtors was still several decades away, as was the abolition of imprisonment for debt. Save for seamen, who were not relieved from their compulsory labor obligations until federal legislation in the twentieth century, liberal insolvency laws by the 1830s virtually had ended specific performance of labor contracts by white workers.

II

Aside from the usual category of debtors, whether from trade or as farm mortgagors, there was a substantial body of indentured servants, largely redemptioners, who were bound to labor for years as determined by written agreements or by the custom of the respective colony or state in return for passage from Europe. In effect, they were contract laborers. Outcroppings of protest arose against a system riddled with fraud. It separated families; imported women on occasion for immoral purposes; and exploited labor, largely unskilled farm labor, without any wage payments except freedom dues at the end of the servant's term—usually a suit of clothes, a gun, and a hoe. With the heavy wave of immigration following the coming of peace, a substantial number of the new arrivals came as redemptioners, although the numbers declined as a multitude of free workers deluged the labor market, and hired hands became an integral part of the economy. However, vestiges of the redemptioner traffic still could be found in Pennsylvania, Delaware, and Maryland well into the 1830s.

At least apprentices to trades, who now faced serious competition from "green hands," including women and children used in the factory system, might take comfort from the prospect of expanded business activity anticipated as a result of the establishment of the new federal government. Contrariwise, bound servants discovered no tangible benefits from the two great national charters of 1787—the Northwest Ordinance and the Constitution. Each made a special point of protecting the property of masters in their servants. While barring slavery and involuntary servitude in the new territory (a prohibition honored in the breach so far as white servants were concerned), the Northwest Ordinance provided that "any person escaping into the same from whom labor service is lawfully claimed in any one of the original States" might be lawfully reclaimed (Article VI).

Article IV of the Constitution contains a similar provision for the return of persons escaping from labor service, while the so-called Fugitive Slave Law of 1793 nailed down the details of enforcement. In sum, the protections that the new national government provided were those for property owners, not for bound workers, white or black. Even when in later years imprisonment for debt was technically abolished, except for fraud, forms of debt servitude and contract labor continued to survive or surface well into the nineteenth century and in some instances much later.

The pool of white labor was swollen by two types of convict labor. The first, which attempted to resurface after the Revolution, comprised persons convicted of crimes or felonies in England, Scotland, and Ireland, and transported to the colonies for long terms; the second, of persons who were sentenced in the colonies to labor service in lieu of satisfying penalties exacted for a variety of crimes, mostly against property. In the six decades before the American Revolution, some 30,000 convicts were transported to America, more than two-thirds of whom went to the Chesapeake colonies.[9] Despite hostile community feeling, convict shipments continued so long as employers thought it profitable to exploit their labor.[10]

Another category of convict servants ranked among the forgotten people. This group comprised persons convicted of a variety of crimes under state laws, including larceny, arson, and bastardy. Traditionally, such malefactors had been sentenced by colonial courts to corporal punishment and to make multiple restitution of the value of the property stolen or damaged. Since the prisoner invariably was unable to make such restitution, the convict would become a judgment debtor and as such bound out to service by the court, a system well entrenched in Massachusetts and Pennsylvania during this period, with Indians, free blacks, and white servants customarily receiving heavier sentences to servitude than the rank and file of free whites. Another, and a very substantial, addition to the labor market came from penalizing absentee or runaway servants by requiring them to serve an additional term amounting to as many as ten days for every day's unauthorized leave, a practice notably found in the tobacco states.[11]

Bastardy posed a special problem to early American communities, and the use of servitude for this offense continued down to relatively recent times in some states. The states continued their colonial practices of imposing additional terms of service on women servants for extramarital pregnancy, while selling into servitude the putative father for a four-year term when he defaulted in his obligation to provide a stated maintenance for the illegitimate child until the latter reached the age of twelve. The proceeds of such a sale of labor services were applied to the child's upkeep. In South Carolina the practice was not ended by law until 1847 and in North Carolina not until 1939.[12]

III

The word "welfare" appears twice in the Constitution. The Preamble declares the promotion of "the general Welfare" to be one of the purposes of the new government the Constitution is establishing, and Article I, section 8, empowers Congress to provide for "the general welfare." Does that suggest that it was the intent of the Framers to provide a welfare state, or a welfare program for the indigent poor and the unemployed? If they did, they would have departed radically from the limited range of activities conducted by the Confederation government under the Articles of Confederation. Article IV of that earlier charter declared as its collective purpose "the better to secure and perpetuate mutual friendship and intercourse among the people of the different states of this Union, the free inhabitants of these states—paupers, vagabonds, and fugitives from justice excepted—shall be entitled to all privileges and immunities of free citizens in the several states." The corresponding section of the Constitution, Article IV, section 2 (the comity clause), drops the reference to paupers and vagabonds and simply reads: "The Citizens of each State shall be entitled to all the Privileges and Immunities of Citizens in the several States." Since the states retained the power to determine their own rules of citizenship, though not of naturalization, and since the comity clause always has been interpreted narrowly by the Supreme Court, no conclusive evidence can be discovered of an intent either to develop a nationally enforceable standard of equality or to extend privileges and immunities to the poor and the homeless.[13]

"The day may come," one scholar suggests, "when the general doctrine under the fifth and fourteenth amendments recognizes for each individual a constitutional right to a decent level of affirmative governmental protection in meeting the basic human needs of physical survival and security, health and housing, work and schooling."[14] That time has not yet arrived, although recent generations have seen the federal and state governments making halting moves in that direction. It certainly had not arrived when the Constitution was framed and ratified. Then poverty, pockets of which could be found in every state, was handled by binding out the poor to private persons or housing them in almshouses or workhouses. In rural New England, public auctions of paupers to the lowest bidder resulted in separating families and the constant shifting of indigent persons from location to location, as they often were sold off on a monthly or quarterly basis.[15] This system, both impersonal and inhumane, was found in the other states as well and was perpetuated in the Northwest Territory.

Along with paupers, the authorities lumped into one unsavory category vagrants, transients, and "strollers," any or all of whom could be jailed, dumped in a workhouse, or hired out as laborers for wages. If defaulting, they could be sold at public vendue for terms ranging from six months to a year and a day, a sentence legislated in South Carolina the same year the Constitution was adopted.[16] In Georgia they could be shipped out of the state.[17] However, by the Confederation era, the trend in the larger cities was to place the indigent poor and the temporarily unemployed in workhouses or almshouses, which, as the New York law stated it, also served as a house of correction for "Beggars, Servants running away or otherwise misbehaving themselves, trespassers, Rogues, and *poor people* refusing to work."[18] In sum, the indigent, the homeless, the unemployed, and the transient poor remained state and local concerns long after the Constitution was ratified.

IV

The word "slavery," Abraham Lincoln one day would note, was "hid away in the Constitution just as an afflicted man hides away a wen or cancer which he dares not cut out at once, lest he bleed to death." Lincoln's metaphor was peculiarly appropriate to the framing of the Constitution. Implicitly, rather than overtly, the Constitution recognized slavery through its three-fifths formula for enumeration, its slave trade compromise, and its provision for the return of fugitives "to service or labor." Slavery may have been the subject of heated remarks during the Philadelphia Convention, but nowhere in the final draft of the Constitution does the word "slave," "Negro," or "black" appear. The drafters were guilty of more than negligent omission since, at the time they were debating the issues concerning black people, one-seventh of the population of the Thirteen States was held in slavery, with a sprinkling of free blacks enjoying at best a quasi-freedom.

Indeed, there is no doubt about the readiness of the northern states to cut a deal on the slavery issue in order to preserve the Union. Still, the slavery compromises at the Philadelphia Convention do not accurately reflect the extent of the conflict then being waged between those moved by humanitarian, religious, and Revolutionary impulses on the one hand, and others accepting the necessity of compromise to preserve a Union threatened with division, if not dissolution. Even southerners were found to reflect such humanitarian impulses. That colorful and contentious planter and former slave trader, Henry Laurens, was perhaps the first southerner to avow privately his readiness to apply the ideals of the Great Declaration to the bondsmen and women on his estates.[19]

Even so vaunted a liberal and humanitarian as Thomas Jefferson soon would find that efforts to ameliorate slavery in his own state would go nowhere and, if persisted in, could be politically damaging. We know that he tried unsuccessfully to write into the Virginia constitution of 1776 a provision that "no person hereafter coming into the state would be held in slavery."[20] Not long after, in his original draft of the Declaration of Independence, he had ascribed to George III, among other wrongful acts, his insistence on continuing the external slave trade, only to see it stricken out by his fellow delegates. The record does not show that Jefferson put up any kind of fight to save this rhetorical, if substantively illogical, section.[21] His notes of July 2 state that the clause was stricken "in complaisance to South Carolina and Georgia," adding, "Our Northern brethren felt a little tender for they had been pretty considerable carriers of [slaves]."[22]

Jefferson's antislavery efforts were not yet exhausted, however. In his 1783 draft of a new constitution for Virginia, he provided for the freedom of all children born of slaves after the year 1800, but the proposition was defeated. Again, and shortly thereafter, he attempted to bar slavery in the territories in the first territorial law of 1784, a remarkably democratic and anticolonial document, but his proposal was defeated by one vote, the delegates voting by states.[23] "The fate of millions of unborn," Jefferson would later comment, "was hanging on the tongue of one man, and heaven was silent in that awful moment." Thereafter, he proved much more ambivalent on the slavery issue. In his *Notes on the State of Virginia* in 1785, he continued to favor gradual emancipation, while failing to include any such program in the revision of his own state's laws. Whether Jefferson was conscious of his deepseated anti-Negro feelings, which found expression in his view about the mental inferiority of the blacks, or whether as a political realist and later national party leader he yielded to conventional opinion, are arguable propositions to which numerous historians have addressed themselves.[24]

One must concede that the Revolution acted as a spur to the manumission of slaves in the South as well as the North, in most cases the beneficiaries of such freedom being the elderly, the infirm, and persons of mixed blood. Owners of such bequests by will frequently avowed that they were prompted by reasons of humanity and conscience, and they sometimes made respectable provisions for the well-being of their manumitted slaves. In general, however, laws enacted in the South permitting manumission usually were designed to prevent the master from shifting support of unwanted free blacks to the public. Since self-hiring was considered a device to circumvent curbs on manumission or an initial step to freedom, the practice usually was frowned upon by city ordinances and state laws, but the prohibitions still were evaded.

In short, aside from a few timid steps taken and the actions of individual slaveowners motivated by humanitarian impulses, the South during the years of the Confederation did little to ameliorate the condition of slavery. Instead of loosening the shackles, the South in most cases tightened such loopholes as existed. Instead of slavery declining in the Upper South, a myth to which some historians have continued to cling, there is a considerable body of evidence to the contrary.[25]

Indubitably, the sentiments voiced in the manumission instruments of these years could be matched by the proslavery petitions addressed in 1784 and 1785 to the Virginia General Assembly. The 1,244 signatures attached to these petitions evidence considerable opposition to manumission and overt hostility to the efforts of Quakers, Methodists, and others to ameliorate the condition of the blacks. To these petitioners there was nothing hypocritical about their Revolutionary rhetoric in stressing property rights and liberty while denying such rights to the black population.[26] As such petitions and much other documentation underscore, most southerners consistently regarded black men and women as outside the constituency and not included in the phrase "all men are created equal."

Turning to the North, a different and more complex set of attitudes is found. Largely as a result of promanumission organizations, whose leadership was primarily Quaker and Federalist, five northern states, in addition to Vermont, which acted prior to its admission to the Union, initiated programs of manumission before the Convention assembled in May 1787. Two other states followed soon thereafter. The antislavery activities were favored not only by their elitist leadership, including Hamilton, Benjamin Franklin, and John Jay, but also by factors of demography and the labor market. Of the northern states only New York had a substantial black population. Free labor was increasingly available and resentful of slave competition. The public authorities encouraged the white population to settle and guard the frontiers, while racial undercurrents, such as fear of miscegenation, by no means should be discounted. Slavery disappeared at a faster rate where blacks made up a proportionately smaller segment of the population. Contrariwise, where the slave population was relatively substantial, notably in New York, manumission was tenaciously resisted. Of the states that adopted gradual emancipation statutes, New Jersey delayed the effects of abolition the longest, while its neighbor to the south, Delaware, maintained slavery even after the Civil War. As late as February 8, 1868, both houses of the Delaware legislature, by joint resolution, rejected a proposed amendment to the state constitution prohibiting slavery or involuntary servitude, and, despite the fact that the Thirteenth Amendment had become a part of the organic law of the land on December 18, 1865, the sale of free Negroes persisted beyond that date in Delaware.[27] Obviously, although Delaware had adopted a limited manumission law in 1787, the egalitarian impulse of the Revolutionary generation stirred not even a ripple in that state.

It was one matter for northern states to adopt measures ending slavery; it was another to carry them out. For example, Pennsylvania, the first state to pass a law for the gradual abolition of slavery, listed the ownership of some slaves as late as the census of 1840. Nor did the bill of rights affixed to New Hampshire's constitution of 1783 immediately bring slavery to an end in that state. Approximately one hundred and fifty slaves were reported in the New Hampshire census of 1790, after which the numbers shrank rapidly. There were still about one thousand slaves in Rhode Island in 1790, underscoring the "gradual" nature of that state's emancipation act of 1784. Despite the Quock Walker Case in Massachusetts, wherein Chief Justice William Cushing held that slavery was "as effectively abolished as it can be" by the assertion in the state's bill of rights "that all men are free and equal; and that every subject is entitled to liberty,"[28] slaves continued to be bought and sold in Massachusetts. Gradually the institution disappeared, either because the blacks now considered themselves free and quit their masters, or because nervous owners disposed of their human property to southern purchasers. By 1790 it had totally disappeared.

In New York, despite the valiant efforts of the New York Manumission Society, organized in 1785, every step toward emancipation was contested. The proposition to free the slaves, put forward by Jay and Gouverneur Morris at the time of the drafting of the Constitution of 1777, disappeared from the final draft; the proslavery forces, largely Anti-Federalist, held off gradual emancipation until July 4, 1799, when a Federalist governor, the committed antislavery leader Jay, signed the legislative measure.[29]

Pregnant with historical potentialities were the antislavery lobbying efforts of the Pennsylvania and New York Manumission societies in the summer of 1787. On June 2 the Pennsylvania Society, probably at the initiation of its secretary, Tench Coxe, memorialized the Convention to suppress the African slave trade, and a similar petition was drafted by the New York Society's president, Jay. Knowing firsthand the sentiment of the southern delegation on the slavery issue, Franklin, the Pennsylvania Society's president, suggested that the petition be let to "lie over for the present."[30] In turn, Hamilton, who had taken leave of the Convention some weeks before but had attended enough sessions to gauge the temper of the delegates on this supersensitive issue, seems to have persuaded the New York Society to withhold its petition.[31] This was a lull before the storm. Hardly had the first Congress, under the new federal government, begun its sessions when that body was confronted with petitions from antislavery groups, the first of these bearing the signature of Franklin.[32] One day a rivulet would flood its banks and not be harnessed.

On the national level, however, the antislavery movement did score one notable victory—the inclusion by the Continental Congress of a provision in the Northwest Ordinance, lifted from Jefferson's earlier effort and moved on the floor by Nathan Dane, prohibiting slavery in the territories north and west of the Ohio. Almost at the very moment this vote was recorded, the delegates in Philadelphia were fashioning a series of compromises on slavery to avoid offending the sensibilities and to secure the votes of their southern collaborators.[33]

What is especially revealing about popular opinion on this issue is the fact that, save for Rhode Island, which was late in coming into the Union and in 1790 proposed a constitutional amendment condemning the slave trade, not one ratifying convention submitted, among the several hundred amendments proposed, a single one dealing with slavery. Rather, one finds that the humanitarian impulse, however spiritedly advanced by abolitionist groups in the North, had limited impact in the free states in the years following the Constitutional Convention. Instead, the decades were marked by the passage of discriminatory legislation that kept free Negroes in the North in a status of quasi-bondage, barred them in most states from the polls and the militia, and managed to keep them off juries, while even barring their entry in some states. Segregation was widespread.[34]

When, in the March 25, 1820, issue of his antislavery journal, *The Philanthropist*, Elisha Bates asserted that a "system of oppression is in full force against the man of color in the free states," he stood on solid ground. In the South, it goes without saying, the humanitarian impulse did not survive the Revolutionary era. Only a few years following the adoption of the Constitution, the cotton gin and the use of long-staple or sea-island cotton fastened slavery on the South and Southwest, with a steady stream of slave manpower moving from the Upper South.[35]

The Revolutionary impulse had shriveled, and that "dark gloominess hanging over the land," which John Woolman had perceived before the American Revolution began, still permeated American society both in the so-called free states and in the rest, more firmly attached than ever to their "peculiar institution."

V

The brief reference to the Indians in the Constitution scarcely suggests the magnitude of the problem Native Americans posed to the nation's security and expansion, or the difficulties confronting the Indians in obtaining equitable treatment at the hands of competing sovereignties—Congress and the states. The Constitution grants Congress the power "to regulate commerce with foreign nations, and among the several States, and with the Indian tribes" (Article I, section 8). Save for the clause dealing with apportionment and direct taxes, excluding Indians "not taxed," the Constitution mentions them nowhere else.

At the Philadelphia Convention, Madison, who long had been irked by the ambivalent powers over the Indians granted under the Articles, proposed a more explicit provision, one that would confer upon Congress the power "to regulate affairs with the Indians as well within as without the limits of the United States." But, by the time his proposal emerged from committee, it was reduced to the simple phrase, "and with the Indian tribes."[36] To this phrasing there was no recorded dissent. Terse and even cryptic as the phrase reads, Congress assumed thereunder the power to legislate trade and intercourse with the Indians. This supremacy over the states in Indian affairs was buttressed by the role the Constitution gives the Senate in treaty making and by Congress's war powers.[37]

After their experience in war and postwar years at the hands of western settlers and the states, the Indians might have been expected to welcome the apparent assertion of paramount authority over their affairs by the new federal government. By bad luck or miscalculation the Indians, with few exceptions, had allied themselves with the British against the Patriots. Hence, most white inhabitants, especially the frontier settlers who had experienced firsthand the ferocity of Indian warfare and had retaliated in kind, shared the view that the Indians deserved no more consideration than did the Loyalists, whose lands had been forfeited and many of whom had been forced into exile. In most states they were denied civil rights and the right to vote.[38]

Persistent tension in Indian-white relations was exacerbated by a growing disparagement of Indian life and culture and a deeply negative view of the potentialities for the assimilation or amalgamation of the Indians. With few notable exceptions, among them Jefferson, Jay, and Anthony Benezet, the Founding Fathers reflected the racist notions of the general public.[39]

In *The Federalist* No. 3, Jay noted that "not a single Indian war has yet been occasioned by the aggressions of the present Federal government, feeble as it is, but there are several instances of Indian hostilities having been provoked by the improper conduct of the individual States, who either, unable or unwilling to restrain or punish offences, have given occasion to the slaughter of many innocent inhabitants." Jay obviously had in mind the massacre of the Christian Indians at Gnadenhutten in Ohio in 1782, and, in response, the torture and murder of Colonel William Crawford by the Delaware some months later.[40] Frontier tension reached its apex during the Convention, with Secretary of War Henry Knox reporting on July 18, 1787, that a war with the Creek and Cherokee tribes was imminent due to violations of the tribe's hunting grounds reserved to them in federal treaties.[41]

From the Indians' point of view the full extent of the tragedy of the late war had become evident with the signing of the Preliminary Articles of Peace in Paris on November 30, 1782. Although Britain, France, and Spain each in turn had sought to curb American expansion, ostensibly out of concern for the Indians, no mention of the Indians can be found in the Preliminary Articles or in the Definitive Treaty of the following year. Instead, the British ceded to the United States lands occupied in substantial part by the Indians as far west as the Mississippi, as far north as the Great Lakes, and as far south as the northern border of the Floridas, which Spain regained.[42] Neither during the peace negotiations nor in the ratification of the treaty by Congress were the Indians ever consulted. Once the Preliminaries were signed, the British officials in America who dealt with the Indians tried to keep the terms of the treaty from them, but the news spread and aroused both indignation and apprehension among Britain's loyal allies.

The perceived need of white Americans for a national Indian policy had deep roots. One may trace it at least as far back as Franklin's Albany Plan of Union of 1754, which would have conferred upon the "President-General" exclusive regulation of Indian affairs. The problem sparked the Royal Proclamation of 1763 and the setting up of superintendents of Indian affairs for the northern and southern departments. Between the Indians and the ever expanding white settlers stood the royal government, presumably as the former's protector. With a fighting rather than a declared war between England and its colonies under way, the Continental Congress, on July 12, 1775, had set up three departments to manage Indian affairs, "to preserve peace and friendship" with the said Indians, and to prevent their taking any part in the present commotions."[43]

When drafts for the Articles of Confederation initially were proposed in the Continental Congress, first Franklin and then Dickinson would have conferred complete jurisdiction over Indian affairs upon Congress, but in its final form the Articles contained a germ of ambiguity, which bedeviled relations between Congress and the states over Indian affairs for the entire span of the Confederation. Thus, Article IX, clause 1, granted Congress the "sole and exclusive right and power of determining peace and war...[and] entering into treaties and alliances." However, clause 4 of the same article, while presuming to reinforce the previous provision giving the United States in Congress assembled "the sole and exclusive right and power" of "regulating the trade and managing all affairs with the Indians," added the descriptive phrase "not members of any of the States," and tacked on the proviso that "the legislative right of any State within its own limits be not infringed or violated."[44]

Although some of the states assumed that the descriptive limitations over Indian affairs contained in the final Articles seriously curbed the authority of Congress, that body exercised some bold initiatives during the years of the Confederation. first, to clarify the authority of the federal government vis-à-vis the states, Congress issued a proclamation on September 22, 1783, forbidding "all persons from making settlements on lands inhabited or claimed by the Indians, without the limits or jurisdiction of any particular State, and from purchasing or receiving any gift or cession of such lands or claims without the express authority and direction" of Congress. The Proclamation declared any such purchase or settlement lacking such authority null and void.[45]

Second, in pursuance of its asserted authority over Indian affairs, Congress, through federal commissioners, concluded a series of treaties with the Indians, starting in October 1784 with Fort Stanwix, New York. That treaty, made with the Iroquois Confederacy, included two members, the Oneida and Tuscarora tribes, who had been allies of the United States, while the remaining four had sided openly with the British. The latter were forced to make substantial concessions, including the abandonment of all Iroquois claims to lands in the Old Northwest. In turn, the government guaranteed the territorial integrity of their allies, the Oneida and the Tuscarora; the pledge was never honored. Governor George Clinton of New York disputed the authority of Congress over tribal lands within the borders of the state, tried to obstruct federal agents from concluding with the Indians, despite the fact that Madison, along with the Marquis de Lafayette, attended the sessions, and in defiance of the opinion voiced by Madison at that time upholding Congress's authority to make such treaties.[46] Subsequently, in 1785 and 1788, Clinton coerced the Oneida into turning over Indian title to over 5½ million acres of their aboriginal land, threatening to withhold state protection against trespassers if they persisted in refusing outright sale. Both New York "treaties" were concluded without the consent of the government, or even its participation.[47] In addition, the Confederation government made treaties with the Wyandots and the Cherokee, both in 1785, and the following year with the Shawnee, the Choctaw, and the Chickasaw.[48]

As it moved toward replacing diplomacy for coercion in dealings with the Indians, the federal government in 1786 set up a northern and a southern department for Indian affairs to execute "such regulations as Congress shall, from time to time, establish respecting Indian affairs," and asserting exclusive power over trade with the Indian tribes.[49] A further step was taken in the spring of 1787 when, at Jay's prodding, Congress adopted a supremacy resolution, holding treaties of Congress binding on the entire nation.[50] The term "treaties," a later Supreme Court held, applied to Indians as well as "other Nations," basing its authority for negativing state actions contrary to Indian treaties on the supremacy clause of the Constitution (Article VI, section 2), which took as its model the earlier congressional resolution.[51]

A fourth step taken by Congress was the adoption in July 1787 of the Northwest Ordinance, whose Article III provided that "the utmost good faith shall always be observed towards the Indians; their lands and property shall never be taken from them without their consent; and in their property rights and liberty they never shall be invaded and disturbed, unless in just and lawful wars authorized by Congress; but laws found in justice and humanity shall, from time to time, be made, for preventing the wrongs being done to them, and for preserving peace and friendship with them."[52]

Throughout the years of the Confederation the issue of the Indians and their lands proved of continuing concern to Congress, whose protective measures toward the Native Americans were flouted systematically by states, speculators, and impatient settlers. The discussions at the Philadelphia Convention reflected the concern of the leadership over this gnawing problem. True, the reference to Indians in that document may have been tantalizingly terse, but henceforth the new federal government would conduct its business with the Indians on the assumption that its authority in that area now would be undisputed. If ambiguities remained after the adoption of the Constitution, they should have been extinguished by the clear prohibition of state purchases of Indian land contained in the Indian Trade and Intercourse Act of July 22, 1790, and its subsequent reenactments.[53]

The Constitution inaugurated a change in Indian policy, both legal and political. Purchase now replaced conquest, but without extinguishing the government's determination to acquire all Indian lands as far as the Mississippi. A new breed of Americans and a new breed of leaders, in contempt of the Constitution, would achieve in the longer run the wholesale annexation of Indian lands, a ruthless program, one incomparable with notions of amicable Indian-white relations and even with the amalgamation of the Indians into the mainstream of American life.[54]

VI

No woman sat at the Constitutional Convention nor at any state ratifying convention. No woman cast a vote for a delegate to the latter. Still, so deep-dyed an Anti-Federalist as Pennsylvania's George Bryan conceded that the female sex, at least in his state, was pro-Constitution. His explanation was that "they admire General W."[55] That admiration was widely shared by the opposite sex as well and indubitably persuaded many Anti-Federalists to support the new charter of government which it was widely believed George Washington would head. If the cult of personality played a role in public opinion about the Constitution, in the case of women it clearly prevailed over interest.

From "We the People" of the Preamble to the frequent references to "persons," "People," or "inhabitants" in the document itself, a case could be made that the Constitution was gender-blind. In determining the intent of the Framers, however, it would have been helpful if they had given us a hint as to whether their use of the masculine pronoun to describe the president and vice-president and, with one exception, the qualifications of representatives and senators, was employed in a generic sense or was meant to exclude women.[56]

Giving to the Framers the most liberal intention in their use of pronouns, one can argue that the Constitution did not explicitly bar women from federal office, while conceding that the election and even appointment of women to fill national posts were ideas whose time had not yet come. Jefferson, who loathed political conversations with the women of Parisian salons, expressed the hope that "our good ladies...are contented to soothe and calm the minds of their husbands returning ruffled from political debate."[57] When he was president, a hint from Albert Gallatin, his secretary of the treasury, that the chief executive might consider appointing women to public service, evoked this sharp rejoinder from Jefferson: "The appointment of a woman to office is an innovation for which the public is not prepared, nor am I."[58] Had Hamilton been alive, he might well have shared his political opponent's sentiments. *The Federalist* contains only one reference to women, and that is in Hamilton's No. 6, in which he warns his readers of the perils posed to the safety of the state by the intrigues of courtesans and mistresses. Jefferson, who usually did not endorse Hamilton's political views, betrayed a like concern over the wiles women might exercise. At an advanced age he made a point of remarking that even the purest democracies would find it necessary to exclude women from the suffrage "to prevent deprivation of morals and ambiguity of issue."[59]

Such antifeminist prejudices did not evaporate quickly but lasted well into the early national era. So preeminent a bluestocking as Mercy Otis Warren, who corresponded on political issues with Jefferson, Dickinson, and the English historian Mrs. Macaulay Graham, aroused the wrath of the irascible John Adams, whose literary jousting with his wife Abigail over this subject is now legendary. Adams did not take kindly to Mrs. Warren's treatment of him in her *History of the Progress and Termination of the American Revolution,* published in 1805. "History is not the Province of the ladies," he observed caustically, a view in which Mercy's nephew, Harrison Gray Otis, heartily concurred.[60] Adams's insensitivity toward his wife's arguments for political justice was revealed privately to James Sullivan:

> Depend upon it Sir, it is dangerous to open so fruitful a source of controversy and altercation as would be opened by attempting to alter the qualifications of voters; there will be no end of it. New claims will arise; women will demand a vote, lads from twelve to twenty-one will think their rights are not enough attended to, and every man who has not a farthing will demand an equal voice with

any other in all acts of state. It tends to confound and destroy all distinctions, and prostrate all ranks to the common level.[61]

In the republic of John Adams, "distinctions" must not be destroyed and women must know their place.

Since the Constitution laid down no voting requirements but left suffrage qualifications to the states, the latter failed to seize the opportunity at the time of ratification and widen the franchise.[62] On the local level, however, there was a certain degree of ambiguity about franchise qualifications. The New England towns continued to make distinctions upon issues on which "freeholders" and "male inhabitants" might vote. In Adams's own town of Braintree, voting on most issues seems to have been open to "the freeholders and other inhabitants," implicitly permitting women property holders to vote. However, the voter and tax lists of Massachusetts reveal that few women holding taxable estates of significant value continued to exercise the local franchise. As Abigail Adams pointed out, restrictions involving the ownership of property by married women, except in the case of marriage settlements or special arrangements, sharply curtailed the number qualifying. Nevertheless, in New England and in some of the middle states, unmarried women with property, as well as widows of proprietors, did participate in making proprietary decisions.[63] In addition, one finds increasing evidence in the 1780s of taxpaying widows joining men in exercising the right of petition to the state legislatures.[64]

More weighty legislation involving provincial or state issues and elections was restricted to male voters. Women were excluded deliberately from the Massachusetts state franchise, along with slaves and minors, as Theophilus Parsons explained in the *Essex Result* (1778), not only because they were "so situated as to have no wills of their own" but also out of the conviction of the delegates to the state constitutional convention that women should be confined to their housewifely role and not encouraged to engage in "promiscuous intercourse with the world, which is necessary to qualify them for electors."[65]

What was true of Massachusetts was true everywhere, with one exception—New Jersey. The provision of its constitution that "all the inhabitants...of full age...worth fifty pounds" could vote was interpreted to include unmarried women otherwise qualified. Some women pounced upon this loophole and exercised the franchise in local elections held in the 1780s and 1790s. Women's votes in 1797 in favor of the Federalist candidate for the state legislature from Elizabethtown are believed to have affected the outcome of the election.

In 1807, however, following several allegations of fraud, an amendment was passed which took away the privilege.[66] Framers of constitutions in other states, like New York and Georgia, were meticulous about avoiding such loopholes and carefully chose the word "male" to describe a voter's qualifications.[67]

Our concern with the treatment of women in the Constitution and their political rights, or lack thereof, in the states should not lead us to conclude that the status of women was unchanged in this period. Contrariwise, appreciable gains were scored by women in conducting business of their own and in securing access to better education. With the coming of the Revolution, the role of republican motherhood was especially esteemed. Women were recognized as models and teachers of civic virtue. A woman now more easily could obtain a divorce and enjoyed other rights at law which would have been denied her in England at common law. True, these gains were modest, and no decisive breakthrough occurred until the married woman's property reform legislation of the nineteenth century. In fact, the era of the Constitution by no means revolutionized the status of women or conferred upon them equal rights. One must accept the judgment of St. George Tucker, who remarked in the first edition of his *Blackstone's Commentaries,* which he published in 1803: "I fear there is little reason for a compliment to our laws for their respect and favor to our female sex."[68]

So much for the forgotten people of the original Constitution. The history of the Constitution is the story of the ways in which constitutional rights and protections came to be extended to all the excluded groups we have examined, and of how that great charter of governance has been broadened by amendment, judicial interpretation, and practice to underwrite a system of participatory democracy that is still a model for other nations.

NOTES

[1]See, for example, *Chisholm v. Georgia,* 2 U.S. *(Dall.* 419, 471 [1793]).

[2]J. R. Pole, *The Pursuit of Equality in American Society* (Berkeley, 1978), 13.

[3]John Adams to Thomas Brand Hollis, June 11, 1790, and to Samuel Adams, February 4, 1794, in Charles Francis Adams, ed., *The Works of John Adams,* 10 vols. (Boston, 1856), 9:569–71; 1:462.

[4]James Wilson, "Lectures on Law," in Robert G. McCloskey, ed., *The Works of James Wilson,* 2 vols. (Cambridge, MA, 1967), 1:240.

⁵Staughton Lynd and Alfred F. Young, "After Carl Becker: The Mechanics in New York City Politics, 1774–1801," in *Labor History* 5 (1964): 215–24.

⁶Space does not permit inclusion of statistical data which some investigators have interpreted as supporting the thesis that a long-run inequality emerged during the eighteenth century. Admittedly, the rapid increase in the population would decrease the amount of freehold or unoccupied land in settled areas after several generations. Contrariwise, such inequalities may have been mitigated by the improvement in transportation, which would increase the number of markets where one would buy and sell, while encouraging organized efforts to settle farther west. Even there, great variations existed in the quality of land farmed. Caution also must be observed in the reliance on tax lists, since numerous propertyless members of families could look forward to inheriting land. Scholars have used National Archives and Records Service, U.S. Direct Tax of 1798, microcopy (Washington, 1965), among them Lee Saltow and Aubrey C. Land, "Housing and Social Standing in Georgia, 1798," *Georgia History Quarterly* 64 (1980): 450–51. As Bernard Bailyn points out, the Boston tax list covers neither all real property nor all owners of real property and includes neither personal property nor actual income. Bernard Bailyn, *Lines of Force* (Washington, DC, 1975), 14. These areas and issues have been probed by James T. Lemon and Gary B. Nash, by Kenneth A. Lockridge, Allan Kulikoff, G. B. Warden, Bruce M. Wilkenfeld, Billy B. Smith, Dirk Hoerder, Herman Wellenreuther, and John K. Alexander, among others. Noteworthy documentation is provided by Alice R. Jones, "Wealth Estimates for the New England Colonies about 1770," *Journal of Economic History* 32 (1972): 104, and in her massive three-volume statistical study.

⁷Jan W. Schulte Nordholt, *The Dutch Republic and American Independence* (Chapel Hill, 1982), 259–63.

⁸Zephaniah Swift, *A System of the Laws of the State of Connecticut*, 2 vols. (Windham, CT, 1795–96), 1:219.

⁹Richard B. Morris, *Government and Labor in Early America* (Boston, 1983), 324–25n.; A. Roger Ekirch, "Bound for America," *William and Mary Quarterly*, 3d ser. (1985): 188; A. E. Smith, *Colonists in Bondage* (Chapel Hill, 1947); Kenneth Morgan, "The Organization of the Convict Trade in Maryland," *William and Mary Quarterly*, 3d ser. (1985): 202.

¹⁰Morris, *Government and Labor*, 336; Walter Galenson, *White Servitude in Colonial America* (New York, 1981), 124–25.

¹¹See Morris, *Government and Labor*, 345–54.

¹²*South Carolina Stat.* 5:279 (1795); *South Carolina Acts of 1847* (Columbia, 1848), 436, 437; *North Carolina Code* (Durham, 1939), sec. 276. Contrariwise, Virginia in the Confederation and early national years subjected the putative father to a jail term unless he posted security or declared himself insolvent. *Virginia Calendar of Acts, 1776–1801* (Richmond, 1792), 183.

[13]See Pole, *Pursuit of Equality,* 112, 113.

[14]Laurence H. Tribe, *American Constitutional Law: A Structure for Liberty* (Mineola, NY, 1978), 574.

[15]See Benjamin J. Klebaner, "Pauper Auctions: The New England Method of Public Poor Relief," Essex Institute, *Historical Collections* 91 (1955): 1–16.

[16]*South Carolina Stat.* 5:43, sec. 6 (1787). See also Richard B. Morris, "White Bondage in Ante-Bellum South Carolina," *South Carolina Historical and Genealogical Review* 49 (October 1948): 191–207.

[17]*Georgia Colonial Records* 19, pt. 2 (1774), 805; (1782), 165–66; (1786), 376.

[18]*New York Colonial Laws* 3, 645 (author's emphasis).

[19]See Richard B. Morris, ed., *A Letter from Henry Laurens to His Son John Laurens, August 14, 1776* (New York, 1964).

[20]Julian P. Boyd et al., eds., *The Papers of Thomas Jefferson* (Princeton, NJ, 1950–), 1:383.

[21]Compare Dumas Malone, *Jefferson the Virginian* (Boston, 1948), 141, with A. Leon Higginbotham, Jr., *In the Matter of Color* (New York, 1978).

[22]Boyd, *Jefferson,* 1:314–15.

[23]See Francis S. Philbrick, *The Rise of the West* (New York, 1965), 125–27.

[24]See, for example, Winthrop D. Jordan, *White over Black* (Chapel Hill, 1968), 130–36; Donald L. Robinson, *Slavery in the Structure of American Politics, 1765–1820* (New York, 1971), 88–97, passim; David Brion Davis, *The Problem of Slavery in the Age of Revolution, 1770–1823* (Ithaca, 1975), 166–67, 174–84.

[25]See Robert McColley, *Slavery and Jeffersonian Virginia* (Urbana, 1964), 3; Robert W. Fogel and Stanley Engerman, *Time on the Cross: The Economics of American Negro Slavery,* 2 vols. (Boston, 1974).

[26]Frederick T. Schmidt and Barbara W. Willhelm, "Early Pro-slavery Petitions in Virginia," *William and Mary Quarterly,* 3d ser. (1973): 133–46.

[27]Richard B. Morris, "The Course of Peonage in a Slave State," *Political Science Quarterly* 65 (1950): 260–62.

[28]See William O'Brien, "Did the Jennison Case Outlaw Slavery in Massachusetts?" *William and Mary Quarterly* 22 (1960): 219–41; John D. Cushing, "The Cushing Court and the Abolition of Slavery in Massachusetts," *American Journal of Legal History* 5 (1961): 118–43.

[29]See Arthur Zilversmit, *The First Emancipation: The Abolition of Slavery in the North* (Chicago, 1967), 146–50; Edgar J. McManus, *A History of Negro Slavery in New York* (Syracuse, 1966), 163–66, 175n.

[30]Pennsylvania Abolitionist Society, ser. 1, reel 2, Minutes, July 2, 1787, Pennsylvania Historical Society.

[31]Richard B. Morris, ed., "John Jay: Confederation and Union," Unpublished Papers, 1784–1789, 3 (New York, 1986).

[32]Jacob E. Cooke, *Tench Coxe and the Early Republic* (Chapel Hill, 1978), 149; *Annals of Congress,* 1st Cong., 2d sess., 1197–1205, 1410–15, 1474.

[33]On a possible deal over this issue, see Staughton Lynd, *Class Conflict, Slavery, and the United States Constitution* (Indianapolis, 1967).

[34]Leon F. Litwack, *North of Slavery* (Chicago, 1961).

[35]Michael Mullin, ed., *American Negro Slavery: A Documentary History* (Columbia, SC, 1976), 126.

[36]Max Farrand, ed., *The Records of the Federal Convention* 3 vols. (New Haven, 1927), 1: 315; 2: 321. Madison had Georgia specifically in mind as a violator of treaties with the Indians in his "Preface to Debates," ibid. 3:548. Indeed, Georgia's prompt ratification of the Constitution seemed to have been sparked by its recognition that an "effective Government" would give Georgians aid against the Creeks. Randolph C. Downey, "Creek-American Relations, 1782–1790," *Georgia Historical Quarterly* 21 (1937): 172–73.

[37]Marshall, C.J. in *Worcester v. Georgia* (6 *Peters* 559). See also Felix S. Cohen, *Handbook of Indian Law* (Charlottesville, 1982), 209–28.

[38]The exclusion of Indians and blacks from voting in the draft Constitution of 1778 was a target of criticism in Massachusetts towns, and the provision was written in the 1780 document. See W. Paul Adams, *The First American Constitutions* (Chapel Hill, 1980), 81, 184–88; Oscar and Mary Handlin, eds., *The Popular Sources of Political Authority: Documents on the Massachusetts Constitution of 1780* (Cambridge, MA, 1966), 231–32, 248–49.

[39]For example, the Massachusetts Act of 1786 proscribing Indian-white marriages proved a model for later New England legislation. See Alden T. Vaughan, "From White Man to Redskin," *American Historical Review* 87 (1982); Reginald Horsman, "American Indian Policy in the Old Northwest, 1783–1800," *William and Mary Quarterly* 18 (1961): 49; Daniel J. Boorstin, *The Lost World of Thomas Jefferson* (New York, 1948), chap. 2; Bernard Sheehan, *Seeds of Distinction: Jeffersonian Philanthropy and the American Indian* (Chapel Hill, 1975).

[40]Randolph C. Downes, *Council Fires on the Upper Ohio* (Pittsburgh, 1969), 271–74; Milo M. Quaife, "The Ohio Company of 1782," *Mississippi Valley Historical Review* 17 (1930–31): 519.

[41]Worthington C. Ford et al., eds., *Journals of the Continental Congress, 1774–1789* (hereafter cited as *JCC*), 34 vols. (Washington, DC, 1904–37), 32: 365–69.

[42]Richard B. Morris, *The Peacemakers: The Great Powers and American Independence* (New York, 1956); Barbara Graymont, *The Iroquois in the American Revolution* (Syracuse, 1972), 259; Wilcomb E. Washburn,

The Indian in America (New York, 1975), 146–65. On the controversial issue as to whether the cession was made to Congress or to the states, see Joseph Story, *Commentaries on the Constitution of the United States*, 3 vols. (Boston, 1833), secs. 198–217, 229–42; more recently, Francis S. Philbrick, *The Rise of the West* (New York, 1965), 114.

[43]*JCC* 11, 174–77.

[44]Ibid. 9: 844–45. Article XIV of the Dickinson draft gave Congress the authority to purchase any Indian lands for the benefit of the colonies; authority to determine western territories was asserted in Article XVIII. The landed states opposed the latter proposition, but Virginia was prepared to grant Congress control over Indian affairs save for "tributary Indians living in and subject to the laws of the state." *JCC* 15: 1076–79.

[45]*JCC* 25: 602.

[46]Gaillard Hunt, ed., *The Writings of James Madison*, 9 vols. (New York, 1900–10), 1: 109–10; Franklin B. Hough, *Proceedings of the Commissioners of Indian Affairs* (Albany, 1861), 21, 22. Later, in *The Federalist*, when Madison was anxious to emphasize the weaknesses of the Confederation government under the Articles, he took a more ambivalent position.

[47]Graymont, *The Iroquois in the American Revolution*, 259 et seq.

[48]See Francis P. Prucha, *American Indian Policy in the Formative Years: The Indian Trade and Intercourse Acts, 1790–1834* (Lincoln, 1962). Indeed, prior to the formal adoption of the Articles of Confederation, Congress had entered into a treaty with the Delaware Nation in 1778, providing passage through their lands and securing soldiers for the Continental Army, in return for which Congress guaranteed the territorial rights of the Delaware and promised to abide by the existing British treaties with the Indians.

[49]*JCC* 21: 491; Prucha, *American Indian Policy*, 36; Horsman, "American Indian Policy," 16–31.

[50]*JCC* 32: 176 (April 13, 1787).

[51]Marshall, C.J. in *Worcester v. Georgia*, 31 U.S. at 559 (1832). It is the argument of claimants in current Indian litigation that the supremacy clause applied to the Confederation treaties and invalidated retroactively state acts inconsistent with and passed subsequently to such treaties. See Joint Brief of Appellants, *Oneida Indian Nation of Wisconsin, Oneida of the Thomas Band, and Oneida Indian Nation of New York v. State of New York et al.*, U.S. Court of Appeals 7616 (1985).

[52]*JCC* 32: 340–41.

[53]1 *U.S. Stat.*, 137.

[54]Horsman, "American Indian Policy," 35–53.

[55]George Bryan, "Account of the Adoption of the Constitution," Bryan Mss., Pennsylvania Historical Society, Philadelphia.

[56]Thus, the Twenty-fifth Amendment on the presidential succession, ratified as recently as 1967, employs the male pronoun throughout to describe the office of the presidency.

[57]Thomas Jefferson to Martha Jefferson, November 28, 1783, and Thomas Jefferson to Nathaniel Burwell, March 14, 1818, in Boyd, *Jefferson Papers* 6:359–61; and Paul Leicester Ford, ed., *The Writings of Thomas Jefferson*, 10 vols., letterpress ed. (New York, 1892–99), 9: 151, 193.

[58]Thomas Jefferson to Albert Gallatin, January 13, 1807, in Ford, *Writings* 9: 7.

[59]Thomas Jefferson to Nathaniel Burwell, March 14, 1818, ibid. 10: 104–6.

[60]"Warren-Adams Letters," Massachusetts Historical Society, *Collections* 72 (1917): 361 et seq.; 73 (1925): 380. See also Abigail Adams to John Adams, March 31 and May 7, 1776, in L. H. Butterfield et al., eds., *Adams Family Correspondence*, 4 vols. (Cambridge, MA, 1963–73), 1: 370, 402–3. Margaret Livingston to Catharine W. Livingston, October 20, 1776, Ridley Papers, Massachusetts Historical Society, Boston.

[61]John Adams to James Sullivan, in Charles Francis Adams, ed., *The Works of John Adams, Second President of the United States: With a Life of the Author*, 10 vols. (Boston, 1850–56), 9: 375–78.

[62]Article I, section 2, provides that the representatives shall be chosen by the electors of each state having the qualifications of the electors of the most numerous branch of the state legislature.

[63]See Joan Hoff-Wilson and Albert L. Sachs, *Sexism and the Law: A Study of Male Beliefs and Legal Bias in Britain and the United States* (New York, 1979), 417–19. Examples may be cited from Samuel A. Bates, ed., *Records of the Town of Braintree, 1640 to 1793* (Randolph, MA, 1886), 509; W. A. Davis, *The Old Records of the Town of Fitchburg*, 6 vols. (Fitchburg, MA, 1898), 1: 39, 115, 214, 280; A. A. Lowell, *Worcester in the War of the Revolution* (Worcester, MA, 1876), 116; Worcester Society of Antiquity, *Bulletin* 16 (1898): 373–78, 451, 452. For women voting on church matters, see Edward J. Brandin, *The Records of the Town of Cambridge, Massachusetts, 1693–1702* (Cambridge, MA, 1930), 68, 69; Francis E. Blake, *History of the Town of Princeton, Massachusetts*, 2 vols. (Princeton, MA, 1915), 1: 136. See also Rosemary S. Keller, *Abigail Adams and the American Revolution* (New York, 1982), 160, 161.

[64]Examples from Virginia are found in C. Bayley, *Popular Influence on Public Policy: Petitioning in Eighteenth-Century Virginia* (Westport, 1979), p. 44.

[65]*Result of the Convention of Delegates Holden at Ipswich in the County of Essex* (Newburyport, MA, 1778), 28, 29. Of all the Massachusetts towns, Northampton alone considered it necessary to explain why "infants" and "women" were excluded, defending its position with a summary reference to John Locke's treatment of "paternal power" and to the *Essex Result*. Handlin, *Popular Sources*, 36.

[66] Mary Philbrick, "Women's Suffrage in Revolutionary New Jersey," New Jersey Historical Society, *Proceedings* 57 (1939): 87–98.

[67] This merely conformed to colonial practice. See Albert E. McKinley, *The Suffrage Franchise in the Thirteen English Colonies in America* (Philadelphia, 1905), 473; Eleanor M. Boatwright, "The Role and Civil Status of Women in Georgia, 1783–1830," *Georgia Historical Quarterly* 30 (1941): 301–24.

[68] The issue has been probed in a number of recent studies on women's role in the period, including Linda K. Kerber, *Women of the Republic: Intellect and Ideology in Revolutionary America* (Chapel Hill, 1980), chaps. 7, 9; Nancy Cott, *Bonds of Womanhood: Women's Place in New England, 1786–1835* (New Haven, 1977); and Suzanne Lebsock, *The Free Women of Petersburg: Status and Culture in a Southern Town, 1784–1860* (New York, 1984).

Commentary to Richard Morris

Yolanda T. Moses

Professor Morris's remarks are both refreshing and significant. He points out that the Twenty-fifth Amendment to the Constitution, which provides for presidential succession and was ratified as recently as 1967, employs the male pronoun throughout to describe the office of the presidency. (Is the male pronoun, used in the eighteenth and twentieth centuries, sufficiently generic and gender-free to provide full access to even the highest office in the land?) Particularly instructive is Morris's clear demonstration that the Federalists (those who supported the Constitution during and following 1787) were rather more liberal than the Anti-Federalists (those who opposed the Constitution). For example, the Federalists were more likely to oppose slavery, while the Anti-Federalists were more likely to approve it.

This last observation is but a footnote to a broader contribution made by Professor Morris. The traditional debate surrounding the origins and purpose of the Constitution, both among scholars and lay persons, often has revolved around the thesis presented early in this century by historian Charles Beard, who has argued that the Constitution of 1787 was purposely designed to turn back the democratic and liberal impulses of the great Declaration of 1776, that the Founders were anti-Revolutionary conservatives wishing above all to protect their property interests against the "people," and that they were commercial urban dwellers opposed to agrarian interests. Beard, influenced by Karl Marx, developed a power-elite thesis regarding the constitutional origins of this Republic; he saw the opponents of the new document as the radical, democratic maintainers of the Declaration's egalitarianism.

Scholarship since Beard's time has done serious damage to his assertions. Students of the period have found that the Constitution makers tended to be younger than their Anti-Federalist opponents, many having commenced their public careers in the Revolutionary

42

movement of the 1770s. Moreover, opponents of the Constitution were as likely to be large property holders as were proponents. At least among white men, the right to vote was probably more widespread than anywhere in the world in the eighteenth century, and in many instances agrarian interests supported the new Constitution.

Perhaps it is time for us to consider the Constitution, not in traditional class terms as suggested by Beard, but rather as a document that, although written by white men, was written for a country with a most varied group of people including women, blacks, Native Americans, and indentured servants. Professor Morris's emphasis on the forgotten people helps us refocus on the Constitution in ways that may be more meaningful for our own time and, indeed, may be more relevant to our peculiar nation. After all, America is made up of a variety of people, all seeking to participate in meaningful ways in this polity.

Morris notes in his final paragraph that our "charter of governance has been broadened by amendment, judicial interpretation, and practice to underwrite a system of participatory democracy which is still a model for other nations." This statement deserves careful reflection and further explication, which can be aided by two events: the celebration of the birthday of Martin Luther King, Jr., and the current unrest in South Africa.

Dr. King spoke and acted in most eloquent ways for the inclusion of forgotten people in the mainstream of American life. In fact, he and his movement were able to utilize the Constitution in their long and difficult but not yet consummated struggle. South Africa at the present has no basic document that can be used so effectively by excluded groups; the words of South African law are clearly exclusive. The struggle there simply does not have the benefit of any conventional protection.

These examples raise two questions: Is the U.S. Constitution a reasonable model for South Africa (or for that matter other nations with a history of denying large groups of people the right of political participation); and, must violence and bloodshed always precede inclusion of formerly excluded groups in political systems? Another way to look at this is to ask a third question: How important are words (as the words of the Constitution) compared to actions (as the actions of powerful people bent on maintaining power whatever words may say)? Can words cause or effect real progressive change?

Returning to Dr. King and what we have come to call the civil rights movement, it is arguable that the successes achieved by this movement were made possible by the Civil War, a bloody episode in our history. The Civil War amendments to the Constitution, made possible by the victory of the Union, provided the constitutional basis for broadened political participation as well as protection of individual rights. For example, the Fourteenth Amendment, with its remarkable definition of citizenship (which is all-inclusive, irrespective of race, sex, or anything else) and its insistence on individual rights, due process of law, and equal protection of the laws, provides the constitutional fodder not only for broad voting rights but also for the desegregation of American society. The famous 1954 Supreme Court case, *Brown v. School Board of Topeka,* used the Fourteenth Amendment. Thus, the Civil War tied the knot that began with the Declaration of Independence and achieved high promise with the Constitution. But that is the point: the Constitution is not a static document; it also is a promise.

Witness further the constitutional amendments and statutory acts that have expanded considerably the most fundamental act of participation, the right to vote:

1) By the late 1820s most states had eliminated property qualifications for white males.
2) In 1870 the Fifteenth Amendment to the Constitution forbade states to deny the right to vote because of "race, religion or previous condition of servitude."
3) Women gained the right to vote with the Nineteenth Amendment in 1920.
4) In 1964 the Twenty-fourth Amendment prohibited states from requiring a poll tax.
5) The Voting Rights Act, passed by Congress and signed by President Lyndon Johnson in 1965, provided for the replacement of local election officials by federal registrars in areas in the South where blacks often were denied their right to vote.
6) The Twenty-sixth Amendment in 1971 forbade states to deny the vote to any citizen eighteen years of age or older.

Consequently, in the two hundred years that our Constitution has been in effect, the franchise has expanded to include virtually everyone over seventeen years of age.

The Declaration of Independence was a magnificent statement about equality. The Constitution provided a magnificent instrument of government, and the history of our society, sometimes bloody, sometimes wanting, has nonetheless, however gradually, insisted that the Declaration and the Constitution merge. The Founders, whatever their contemporary views about blacks, women, debtors, and Native Americans, left us the essential words for this historic enterprise.

Still—and very important—as Professor Morris has hinted, the Founders foresaw a nation not homogeneous with simple majority rule. They, as should we, understood the problems of rule by a like-minded, pure majority. Despite all, they envisioned a nation of variety, a nation that could incorporate even forgotten people.

James Madison, in his famous *The Federalist* No. 51, wrote that "in a free government the security for civil rights must be the same as that for religious rights. It consists in the one case in the multiplicity of interests, and in the other in the multiplicity of sects. The degree of security in both cases will depend on the number of interests and sects." He welcomed a society of diversity. Indeed, although Madison well might not recognize the diversity we have today, he would argue that we need many kinds of people and interests.

The richness, diversity, and complexity of American life may pose some of our greatest problems, but they also are sources of much of our strength and vitality as a nation. "I hear America singing," wrote Walt Whitman, "the varied carols I hear."

Forgotten people could not long be forgotten in a country willed into existence by Founders who believed that human beings, equal in nature, could devise governments without the aid of divinity, kings, or accident. We may still have deprivation in this country, but we are, unlike South Africa, totally committed to full, broad democratic participation on the part of all of our people. The gift of the Founders was not a parochial social view but the dynamic words of the future.

Expanding Civic Virtue: Participation and the Constitution

Sarah Weddington

It is appropriate in this, the 200th year of our Constitution's origin, to direct our thoughts to the importance of and need for participation in the leadership of this country. We should take more directed and disciplined steps to encourage the development of leadership skills and a feeling of personal responsibility to participate in civic activities, especially among our young people. After all, the Founders of our Constitution knew that a republic could work only if its people demonstrated active public-spiritedness. This is what I mean by civic virtue, and it is as important today as the Founders believed it was in the eighteenth century.

In approaching the issue of civic virtue, I will first share some of my experiences in the judicial and executive branches of our government, then focus on the need for civic participation and public leadership in order to sustain the form of government envisioned by the writers of the Constitution, and will conclude by suggesting ways to encourage participation in civic responsibility and leadership.

For many lawyers, arguing a case before the U.S. Supreme Court is the experience of a lifetime. The history of the Court is a tribute to the decisions made by those attending the Constitutional Convention and to their ability to foresee the need for checks and balances among the three branches of government. It is likely that none of us would agree entirely with all of its decisions, but we would agree that it is an institution of novel importance in our nation's history. Its authority has allowed us to live according to fundamental principles established in the Constitution, as amended, rather than swaying to and fro with the natural swings of popular opinion that occur from time to time. The work of the Court is founded on the bedrock of the Constitution.

The Supreme Court building is an awe-inspiring structure composed of thirteen discrete kinds of marble. After ascending the long flight of stairs and entering a marble hallway (after checking any personal belongings and passing security), one steps through velvet curtains into the high-ceilinged and marble-columned courtroom. The pews at the back, much like church pews, are for visitors. The "five-minute section" is for tourists who visit for only moments. Another section is for those who have been waiting in line—often for two or three hours—to hear full arguments of a case. A gold railing separates the laymen from the lawyers.

The day I argued there the visitors' and bar sections were packed. As I passed by them I came to the four tables where those who present cases sit. When the Court hears cases, it hears two in the morning and two in the afternoon. Each case is allocated one hour, one half-hour for each side, although voluminous documents submitted in advance have been studied by the justices. At the counsel table is a souvenir handmade quill pen. To the right is the podium where cases are argued, with what some lawyers call the "cheat sheet" on it, a diagram of the seating arrangements of the justices. A few feet away is the slightly elevated bench where the nine judges sit, each in an individually made chair. The formally dressed clerk of the Court opens hearings declaring: "Oyez, Oyez, all ye please rise and face the Court." The velvet curtains at the back part, and the judges enter. The Chief Justice then asks the attorney to have one of the litigants begin.

The practice of oral argument before the Court does not include explanation of the case to the judges but rather the answering of questions they might have. In my case the questioning was intense, but I left with no inkling of the Court's decision. Later I learned that I had won.

Judicial review, a concept derived from our Constitution and from early Court decisions, gives our Supreme Court a most powerful influence on public life. The Court is not elected, nor does it have an army to enforce its decrees. In a certain sense it remains, as Alexander Hamilton asserted in *The Federalist* No. 78, perhaps the weakest of the three branches. Yet we accept its judgments, and on the whole we tend to find its aloof and rarely invoked power essential for our multifaceted Republic.

Part of the addictive nature of being in Washington is that the levers of power seem larger than elsewhere. For a given amount of time and effort, results appear more visible and influence on the future more likely than anywhere else in the country. This is particularly true for working in the White House, where I served as one of the assistants to President Jimmy Carter. To be part of the decision-making process in the executive branch is to see the effect of various forces in shaping the events about which the public reads and to know that I played a role in some of those decisions. Perhaps as important was the opportunity to meet, visit, and work with leaders from all levels of this country and from other nations.

The presidency is a curious office in modern state politics. Neither king nor prime minister, the president nevertheless is expected to perform the functions of both, and yet, as prescribed by the Constitution, his powers are limited, as virtually all presidents have learned, some to their chagrin. Here, in the executive branch, above all we can see the essence and necessity of leadership in the Republic. Service in the White House underscored the delicate constitutional requirements that both restrain and yet provide for presidential leadership. Persuasion and noble politicking are often essential, as when President Carter successfully maneuvered the Panama Canal treaties through the Senate. Our best presidents have understood constitutional perquisite and restraint, and they have enjoyed the practice of leadership.

It was indeed sad leaving the White House. Tradition calls for the staff of the outgoing president to come to work that last morning, to clean out desks and say goodby to colleagues, and to exit about 11 A.M. in order to go to Andrews Air Force Base, there to wave goodby when their leader departs. Simultaneously, the new people enter; by noon a complete change in the control of the White House has occurred. Upon hearing Ronald Reagan at the inaugural podium declare how fortunate we are to live in a nation where change takes place peacefully and under the rule of law, the sadness at leaving was considerably mitigated. Among the valuable inheritances of the Constitution is that it has withstood the test of time by providing for the will of the people to be expressed and honored in the selection and periodic change of national leaders.

Sorrow at leaving, however, was more than just unhappiness in relinquishing the influence on governance, or saying farewell to the Carters, or giving up my White House pass. I was concerned that the pools of leadership talent did not seem to be as full as they should be. Even at this date, few women hold titles of leadership and, perhaps more ominously, fewer and fewer citizens feel the responsibility of civic participation.

On numerous occasions I have heard concerned people in local situations comment on the difficulty of encouraging people to run for elective office, or head local service organizations, or lead civic projects. Increasingly, we are a people self-engaged, too rarely involved in the larger purposes of our community. How can we encourage people with the talents and the willingness to undertake tasks of civic responsibility? This country was founded by Americans who felt a responsibility to their community. Their dedication provided us with considerable advantages. But there are responsibilities that accompany the privileges of citizenship.

Leaders are our most critical resource. Whether we think of politics, education, business, civic, church, or home activities, all of them are dependent on leaders. Corporations spend vast sums trying to recruit new employees with leadership potential and providing leadership training for current employees. Yet we do not have any comparable training for civic and public leadership.

Some have called youth today the "me" generation. Ernest Boyer and Arthur Levine in *A Quest for Common Learning* emphasize the "'new narcissism,' the self-absorption and myopic obsession with immediate gratification" that characterize recent generations. If the "me" generation has as a primary concern how much money can be made and how much fun and excitement can be crammed into one lifetime, then it may well be missing out on what makes life satisfying in the long run.

We should search actively for ways to encourage all, but particularly those with high potential, to give more of themselves to the rewarding experiences involved in civic activities. This should expand our pool of future leaders.

Many definitions of leadership have been suggested. Harry Truman maintained that "leadership is the ability to get people to do what they don't want to do and like it." Michael Korda has said that "leadership is the ability to set an organization to music, the music to which it will dance." Others have emphasized elements of education, dedication, and inspiration.

Leadership is essentially the ability to work successfully with other people to accomplish a goal. There is no one correct source of leadership. For example, considering who our presidents have been, one sees the impact of trends beyond the characteristics of the candidates. In the early part of this century, candidates and winners came often from positions as governors—the Roosevelts and Woodrow Wilson. The national media then developed, and the focal point was Washington. Our next series of presidents came from Congress—John F. Kennedy, Lyndon Johnson, Richard Nixon, and Gerald Ford. When a public sentiment developed that there was too much power in the nation's capital, presidents once again came from state houses—Carter and Reagan.

The styles of presidents have similarly varied, as with Dwight Eisenhower, who gave the nation a chance to relax after the war effort, and Kennedy, who symbolized its later readiness to make dramatic progress, as in the exploration of space. The Cherokees even had two chiefs, one a war chief and the other a peace chief. The Indians believed that no one person was best suited for both roles.

As for leadership skills, certainly there are those that enhance leadership and can be learned. They include communication skills, goal setting, and human relations. They can be taught in classes or through the use of the critical eye, and they can be improved by practice. However, another skill is also needed—the ability to fail and to try again. We tend to remember people's successes and forget their failures. For example, we remember Abraham Lincoln as the president who preserved the Union, but we forget how many times he lost election contests (indeed, the last campaign he entered before his nomination for president was for the Senate seat from Illinois; he lost to Stephen Douglas). We think of Barbara Jordan as a marvelous woman member of Congress, but we forget that she ran twice and lost before she was first elected. We remember Babe Ruth as the baseball player with the highest number of home runs, but we forget that the same year he also had the highest number of strikeouts. We must teach young people that their future, if they take any risks, will include failures. But these failures are not necessarily fatal; they are to be expected and overcome.

We need to train people to be leaders. We need to call them leaders and make that a part of their self-concept. We need to instill in them an appreciation of the inheritance of leadership our constitutional fathers passed down to us and of the importance of civic leadership and participation today and in the future.

Perhaps we should review our educational system to see if classes can be added or segments of our history and civics classes structured to include an understanding of the eighteenth-century notion of civic virtue—not excessive patriotism, but a loving regard for the common good. Ernest Boyer's *High School* suggests that all high-school students complete a service requirement involving volunteer work in the community or at the school site. Such a requirement would be coupled with a studied awareness of civic duties. We could enhance such undertakings by asking the participation of local leadership programs, such as Leadership Dallas or Leadership Austin, to "adopt" young people with the potential to make a valuable civic contribution.

Currently, we are seeing more efforts to bring women and minority men into a pool of talent that can be tapped for leadership positions. To be honest with those we hope to involve, we must tell them that leadership has a price. Those who wrote the Constitution did not do so amid smooth, harmonious surroundings and with universal acclaim. In fact, many of them had been part of a revolution against constituted authority, and they would draw severe criticism during the ratification debates. There is a cost to leadership. Someone once said that the pioneers take the arrows. But think about the people who might never have thought of themselves as leaders but who, in fact, through their leadership roles have made life better for others. For example, over 90 percent of the libraries in Texas were started by women in the General Federation of Women's Clubs who had a simple belief that people in towns large and small should have access to books.

When we celebrate the Constitution and the rich heritage of freedom, justice, and equality it has provided us, we also must celebrate and remember the leaders who created it. And, when we consider the necessary ingredients to pass on that heritage vital and strong, the first one surely must be public-spirited leaders who are adequate to the task. It is time that we remember and remind others of the civic responsibility that accompanies the privilege of citizenship.

The Preamble to the Constitution says: "We the People of the United States, in order to form a more perfect Union, establish Justice, insure domestic Tranquility, provide for the common defense, promote the general Welfare, and secure the Blessings of Liberty to ourselves and our Posterity, do ordain and establish this Constitution for the United States of America." These are large responsibilities pressed by the Founders on "We the People." We cannot meet them by pursuing simple self-interest. We must have an expanding pool of citizens of civic virtue who are willing to participate in maintaining our highest ideals. We must dedicate ourselves jointly to that task.

Commentary to Sarah Weddington

Charles E. Wiggins

September 17 of each year is generally regarded as the anniversary date of the Constitution, and in 1987 we will celebrate its bicentennial on that day. But that is only the date of its signing by the gentleman from Virginia, George Washington, and thirty-eight of his colleagues who labored during the summer of 1787 in Philadelphia. After its signing, the document was transmitted to the Continental Congress, which had called the Convention by resolution the previous February. The Continental Congress thereupon submitted the proposal—and that is all it was in September 1787—to the states for their ratification. Considering the magnitude of their task and the controversy surrounding this historic document, the three-fourths of the states necessary for ratification acted with uncommon speed. The ninth state, New Hampshire, ratified the proposal on June 21, 1788.

Ratification itself, however, did not create and install a government in America under the new Constitution. The Continental Congress was compelled to implement the structure of the government which the Constitution created. That government did not come into being until March 1789. Our celebration in 1987 is not premature; we have much to remember and much to discuss. Even from now until March 1989 will not be time enough.

The Constitution that we revere today was not considered perfect two centuries ago. Flaws were noted in that historic document, and it has changed. The Constitution celebrated today is the product of two hundred years of evolving and enlightened political, moral, and economic standards. That process continues. The Constitution of two hundred years ago was a magnificent and unprecedented beginning for a society wishing to govern itself. That beginning is worthy of national celebration. The full story of this Constitution, however, requires an understanding of subsequent events, the bicentennial of which are many years in the future.

With particular reference to "participation and the Constitution," Ms. Weddington's career in government in Texas and in Washington was not solely the consequence of her obvious intelligence, coupled with ambition, hard work, and luck. It was a consequence of an evolving governmental structure that permitted her talents to blossom. A Ms. Weddington, in the eighteenth century, could not have served in the legislature of any ratifying state, nor could she have served in the First Congress. She would not have qualified as an elector because she is a woman. It was not until the ratification of the Nineteenth Amendment in August 1920 that the constitutional right of women to vote was assured, finally removing that historic impediment to participation in government.

Oddly, the conscience of our society was not sufficiently aroused to demand political rights for women for more than one hundred thirty years after the ratification of the Constitution, whereas the issue of slavery and unequal rights for blacks plagued our society from the very beginning. Slavery was rooted in the contemporaneous history of our Constitution's founding. At least thirty-five of the fifty-five participants in the Constitutional Convention were slave owners. In a few states, the movement for the abolition of slavery, as a denial of a human right, was growing. In most states, however, and surely in the Convention of 1787, slavery was perceived as an economic issue and as an issue related to the voting power of individual states in Congress rather than as an issue of human rights.

It was not until the three great post-Civil War amendments—the Thirteenth, abolishing slavery; the Fourteenth, requiring that states afford equal protection to their citizens; and the Fifteenth, granting blacks the right to vote—that citizen participation in our government by blacks was given at least nominal recognition. It did not become more than a mere nominal right until much, much later.

Other amendments adopted since the founding have expanded the political rights of our citizens. The Twenty-third Amendment gave residents of the District of Columbia the right to select presidential electors, the Twenty-fourth outlawed the poll tax, and the Twenty-sixth afforded citizens eighteen years old and older the right to vote. To this list of relatively recent amendments which clearly are related to the right of citizen participation in government, one cannot neglect perhaps the most important amendment of all, the First Amendment, ratified in 1791, or the Seventeenth Amendment, providing for the direct election of senators.

The right of citizens to participate in the affairs of their government is rooted in the words of the Constitution, amendments adopted to it, and in several unstated but well-understood concepts of self-government. But a constitution is not self-executing. The words of ours have been given practical meaning on the anvil of cases and controversies resolved by courts bound to apply those words to the facts before them. The cases involving citizen participation in government protected by the First, Fifth, and particularly the Fourteenth, Amendments are legend. For now, let me make passing mention to one line of case only, which is still evolving and which is known popularly as the law of "one person, one vote."

We know that Elbridge Gerry was a delegate to the Constitutional Convention from Massachusetts. We know of his illustrious public career as a member of the First Congress, as governor of Massachusetts, and as vice-president of the United States under James Madison. He signed the Declaration of Independence, but he was one of three delegates to the Convention who could not bring himself to sign the Constitution in 1787.

For all of his distinguished public service, Gerry best may be remembered for his role, as governor, in manipulating the shape of political districts in his state for a partisan objective. He was the father (at least on these shores) of gerrymandering. The consequence of gerrymandering, successfully practiced, is the maintenance of political power at the expense of equality of voting power. For many years the Supreme Court acknowledged the dilution of voting power occasioned by gerrymandering but refused to consider cases challenging it, by invoking a principle of judicial self-restraint known as "justiciability." The courts concluded that political gerrymandering was a political question which by its nature was not justiciable, that is, capable of judicial resolution.

All of that changed in the profound decision of *Baker v. Carr.* Inequality in voting power finally was seen as a justiciable constitutional question involving a denial of equal protection of the laws. One person, one vote was born. Since then, the principle requiring electoral districts to be equal in population has been applied to all manner of electoral districts except the U.S. Senate. Recent cases recognize that the right to vote a ballot of equal weight, and the right to have that ballot counted, is not the be-all and end-all of political participation. The "right to elect" a person of the dominant race or religion of the voters also has been recognized.

Now the Supreme Court is considering an issue of special importance to Californians: does political gerrymandering—that is, a denial of the right to elect a Republican or a Democrat—offend the Constitution? Political gerrymandering is successfully practiced when electoral district lines are so drawn as to assure the dominance of one party and the permanent subjugation of the other as a minority. The right of minority voters "to elect" is thus denied. Needless to say, I express no opinion on this sensitive question.

These cases have had a tremendous and lasting impact upon citizen participation in our government. The results are not solely the consequence of random good ideas. Rather, expanded citizen participation in government is the fulfillment of a political philosophy embraced in our Constitution two hundred years ago, but which eighteenth-century society was not ready to implement. The core of that philosophy was stated simply by Alexander Hamilton in describing the House of Representatives: "Here, sir, the people govern."

In two hundred years we have not found the true, the ultimate, meaning of our Constitution. I mean no offense to strict constructionists to suggest that, in a dynamic society, old phrases surely will be applied to new situations. Although a word or a phrase may be given a new meaning, the basic structural flaws that existed in the beginning have been largely corrected. The need for dramatic changes, such as occurred with the adoption of the Bill of Rights and the Civil War Amendments, has passed and surely will not recur—except one hopes that the ticking political time bomb, the Electoral College, will be defused by amendments requiring the popular election of the president. More relevant to this discussion, the Constitution now provides ample authority for assured citizen participation in our government. As a fitting celebration of the Bicentennial, everyone should be urged to exercise the constitutional rights afforded them and to participate fully in the affairs of government.

Political Parties and Article VIII of the Constitution

Austin Ranney

The title of this paper clearly contains a major blooper. The Constitution of the United States has only seven articles, adopted by the Philadelphia Convention on September 17, 1787, and put into operation on March 4, 1789. Moreover, the only changes in the Constitution have been the twenty-six amendments added at various times from 1791 to 1971.

Most political scientists, however, agree with Walter Bagehot's conviction that a purely literary theory of any nation's constitution—a theory that deals only with words explicitly declared by a formal initiating agency and altered by subsequent formal amendments—misses too much. A constitution so regarded, Bagehot said, is rather like "an old man who still wears with attached fondness clothes in the fashion of his youth: what you see of him is the same; what you do not see is wholly altered."[1] Bagehot's intellectual descendants among present-day political scientists believe that, in all but the narrowest legal sense, a nation's constitution consists of all the fundamental and enduring institutions and rules—written and unwritten, legal and extralegal—by which the nation in fact makes its political decisions.

Many constitutional historians believe that the Bill of Rights, in fact if not in law, was a part of the original Constitution. They point out that several states ratified the Constitution only because pledges were made that such guarantees would be added to the document as the first order of business by the new government. And so they were; the first ten amendments were approved by Congress on September 25, 1789, and ratified by three-fourths of the states by December 15, 1791.

Some historians, indeed, see the Bill of Rights not so much as additions to the original Constitution as its "Article VIII." This is an appealing and even useful conceit, and the thesis here is that this notional Article VIII has more than one "section," and that political parties constitute a section that is at least as important as the Bill of Rights, judicial review, the career bureaucracy, the mass communications media, and other institutions that arguably should be included as parts of the "article."

A Constitution against Parties[2]

Preparty Politics in the 1780s

As long as people have played politics there have been political organizations, for the excellent reason that the players always have found that pooling strength and concerting strategy with like-minded others are the first tactical requirements for success. In most policies until the eighteenth century, however, government decisions were made by absolute monarchs or small oligarchies, and politics consisted largely of backroom intrigues by small groups of competing courtiers known as "cabals," "juntos," "factions," or even "parties." Full-fledged modern political parties first emerged in the United States in the 1790s, and there, as in other nations, they developed in the following five stages:[3]

1) Legislative assemblies acquired some power and standing independent of the monarch.
2) Groups of legislators formed intragovernmental organizations to make strategy and concert action.
3) A significant number of legislators came to be chosen by ordinary citizens in free elections.
4) The intragovernmental organizations stimulated their supporters outside the legislature to form extragovernmental organizations to elect more right-thinking legislators.
5) The leaders of the parties and the general public came to accept the idea that competition and alternation in power by organized political parties are a desirable way of conducting a government whose just power must rest upon the consent of the governed.

When the Founding Fathers met in Philadelphia in the spring of 1787, the new American polity was in stage three of this developmental process. Many state legislators were elected by popular votes (although on restricted franchises), and some of them, as well as some members of the Confederation's Congress, formed semiorganized intragovernmental groups, variously known as "factions," "interests," "cliques," and "parties." Some spoke for mainly economic interests, such as farmers, merchants, and manufacturers, while others represented mainly sectional interests.

As the 1780s wore on, however, an increasing number of political activists outside and inside the legislatures lined up with one side or the other of the overriding dispute between those who wanted a much stronger national government and those who did not. The former were often called "federalists" and the latter "anti-federalists," and, while they were far from being fully formed political parties in 1787, they were the roots from which the world's first modern parties emerged in the early 1790s. It was this kind of organized political competition with which the Framers of the Constitution were familiar. They did not like it very much, and they wrote a constitution that had, as one of its main objectives, to keep such political organizations from, as they saw it, tearing the new nation apart.

The Framers' Attitudes toward Parties

In many respects the men who wrote the Constitution of the United States were English gentry, whose education and attitudes differed significantly from their counterparts in the mother country only on how much autonomy from the Crown should be given to the governments of the new world. Thus, they regarded the new forms of political organization much as the Marquis of Halifax and Viscount Bolingbroke had regarded them in the late seventeenth and early eighteenth centuries. As most of the Framers saw it, competing political organizations are inherently subversive of good government and the national interest. Each works for the interest of only part of the nation (hence the term "party"), their squabbling corrodes national unity and patriotism, and, if one of them manages to get control of the government, it will ruthlessly advance its interest at the expense of all others, especially the national interest.

The most prominent American expression of this widely held view was made by the greatest American of the time. As he approached the end of his lifetime of service to his country, George Washington devoted the bulk of his Farewell Address to warning his countrymen against the ruinous effects of organized political competition. As he put it:

> ...all combinations and associations, under whatever plausible character, with the real design to direct, control, counteract, or awe the regular deliberation and action of the constituted authorities, are...of fatal tendency. They serve to...put, in the place of a delegated will of the Nation, the will of a party;...and, according to the alternate triumphs of different parties, to make the public

administration the mirror of the ill-concerted and incongruous projects of faction, rather than the organ of consistent and wholesome plans digested by common councils, and modified by mutual interests.[4]

Washington's doctrine was widely believed, but the view that shaped the writing of the Constitution was the less conventional and more penetrating analysis set forth by the great constitutionalist James Madison in *The Federalist* papers, especially the tenth—an analysis that many scholars regard as the greatest work of political theory yet set forth by an American. Madison began by endorsing the conventional view that unbridled competition among organized political groups (he called them "factions") means that "our governments are too unstable, that the public good is disregarded in the conflicts of rival parties, and...measures are too often decided, not according to the rules of justice and the rights of the minor party, but by the superior force of an interested and overbearing majority."[5]

Madison went well beyond Washington's simple anathemas. There are, he said, "two methods of curing the mischiefs of faction: the one, by removing its causes; the other, by controlling its effects."[6] Factions/parties arise from the basic desire of human beings to advance their particular interests as effectively as possible, and they are made possible by the Constitution's guaranteed rights of freedom of speech and assembly. Accordingly, the only way to remove their causes entirely is to set aside those rights, and that cure would be far worse than the disease. It is much better, Madison said, to control their effects. But, he asked, "By what means is this object attainable?" And he answered: "Evidently by one or two only. Either the existence of the same passion or interest in a majority at the same time must be prevented, or the majority, having such a coexistent passion or interest, must be rendered, by their number and local situation, unable to concert and carry into effect schemes of oppression."[7]

The first strategy is best pursued by spreading the nation over a large territory and a large population, thereby lessening the chance that one faction will be able to mobilize the support of a majority of all the people everywhere. Accordingly, the more numerous, varied, and dispersed are the nation's interests the safer are the people's rights. In Madison's words:

> Extend the sphere and you take in a greater variety of parties and interests; you make it less probable that a majority of the whole will have a common motive to invade the rights of other citizens; or if such a common motive exists, it will be more difficult for all

who feel it to discover their own strength and to act together in unison with each other.[8]

The second strategy is best pursued by dividing the power of government into a number of parcels and giving each parcel to a separate and independent government agency. This will leave no single lever of power that one faction/party can grasp and thereby the whole might of government to advance its interest at the expense of other interests. As Madison summed it up in the forty-seventh paper:

> No political truth is certainly of greater intrinsic value, or is stamped with the authority of more enlightened patrons of liberty than that . . . the accumulation of all powers, legislative, executive, and judiciary, in the same hands, whether of one, a few or many, and whether hereditary, self-appointed, or elective, may justly be pronounced the very definition of tyranny.[9]

He was confident that under the Constitution this way of curing the mischiefs of faction

> will be exemplified in the federal republic of the United States. Whilst all authority in it will be derived from and dependent on the society, the society itself will be broken into so many parts, interests and classes of citizens, that the rights of individuals, or of the minority, will be in little danger from interested combinations of the majority.[10]

The Antiparty Constitution

On the basis of this political theory, the Founding Fathers designed what was, in Richard Hofstadter's apt phrase, "a Constitution against parties." The new government's power was divided into three great parcels, and each was given to a separate and independent agency selected in a different manner and resting on a different base from the others. The legislative power was divided between two coequal chambers. The members of the House of Representatives were elected by popular votes to serve for two-year terms, and all of them came up for reelection every two years. The members of the Senate were chosen by the state legislatures for six-year terms, and only one-third of them came up for reelection every two years. The executive power, after some disagreement in the Convention, was given to a president chosen by a special Electoral College for a four-year term. The judicial power was given to a Supreme Court whose members were nominated by the president, were approved by the Senate, and served until death, resignation, or impeachment by Congress. Moreover, each of the three branches was given weapons (checks and balances) to preserve its sphere of power against invasion by the other branches; for example, the power of the president to veto acts of Congress, and the power of Congress to establish lesser federal courts and fix their jurisdictions. (One of the most important checks of all—the power of the courts to overturn acts of Congress and the president by declaring them unconstitutional—was not established until 1803 when, in the case of *Marbury v. Madison,* the Supreme Court gave itself the power and thereby added the second section to "Article VIII.")

That was fragmenting power on a grand scale, and we, the Founding Fathers' heirs, should never lose sight of the fact that they did not intend a system that would enable government to do good things. Quite the contrary: they intended a system that would keep government from doing bad things. The implicit major premise of Articles I through VII is that it is better for government not to act at all than to act in a way that will damage the vital interests of any of the nation's major elements. That is still their major premise, but almost from the start the constitutional system was changed significantly by the rather different premises of "Article VIII," especially the section that establishes political parties.

"Article VIII": The Parties Emerge

Why Parties? Why So Soon?

Seldom in history has a political system been so carefully designed by such great constitutional architects. No other written constitution in the world has survived so long. No nation has fared so well. No wonder the great Englishman William Ewart Gladstone called it "the most remarkable work...to have been produced by the human intellect, at a single stroke, in its application to political affairs."[11] Yet it also must be said that seldom in human history has so carefully designed a system undergone such great changes so soon. For the political parties the Framers had wanted to forestall emerged in less than three years after the new government opened its doors, and the chief architect of the Constitution against parties, Madison himself, became one of the two chief architects of the first full-fledged modern party. Why and how did it happen so soon?

The "why" question is easily answered: the political conditions of the time made the emergence of modern parties inevitable. For one thing, the politics of the late 1780s and early 1790s was split along one great faultline, with most politicians and ordinary citizens identified with either the coalition of merchant, trading, manufacturing, and creditor interests headed by Alexander Hamilton and centered in New England, or the coalition of planter, small farmer, and debtor interests headed by Madison and Thomas Jefferson and centered in the South and West. For another, the new Constitution's guarantees of freedom of speech and assembly removed most of the historic barriers against political organization. From the start Hamilton injected the conflict into the new government by pressing his program for funding the state debts, establishing a national bank, and imposing protective tariffs. Moreover, he assiduously cultivated support in Congress and the administration for his program, and his intragovernmental "federalists" soon became so well organized and effective that their label gained a capital "F."

Hamilton's leading opponents, Jefferson and Madison, almost immediately acted upon a universal law of free politics—namely, the first weapon against hostile organization is counterorganization. They formed an association of like-minded members of Congress that came to be known as "the republican caucus." Its members soon realized that Hamilton's designs could be blocked effectively only if more "Republicans"—their label rapidly acquired a capital "R"—were elected to Congress. So they encouraged the formation of extragovernmental organizations, known variously as Democratic Societies and Republican Clubs, in which their supporters in a number of localities assembled, agreed to back particular anti-Hamilton candidates for Congress, and mounted campaigns to get them elected.

As Hofstadter relates, at first the Federalists denounced the new party organizations as subversive, declaring that "the representative institutions of republicanism were in themselves sufficient as instruments of government, and any attempt to set up political clubs or societies outside them would be an attempt not to extend but to destroy republican institutions." But the Hamiltonians too had to face the organizational necessities of free political competition. In Hofstadter's words, "As the exigencies of political opposition impressed themselves upon the Federalists in greater force, they began to found considerable numbers of their own political clubs, [which were called] the Washington Benevolent Societies."[12]

Their Rapid Development

By the election of 1800 the United States had become the world's first nation to move into stage four of the developmental process outlined earlier, and, in William Nisbet Chambers's words, the transition was completed "from the older 'connexions' of fluid factions, family cliques, or juntos to the newer, modern connection of the party."[13] Both national and local politics consisted mainly of the competition for control of the personnel and policies of government by two well-defined organizations, generally called the Federalist and Republican parties. The adherents of each party in Congress met frequently in gatherings known as congressional caucuses, and the Republican members of the House of Representatives chose Albert Gallatin as their floor leader. Both parties' national intragovernmental organizations were well connected with a growing number of extragovernmental organizations of party supporters who chose candidates for national, state, and local offices and campaigned for their election.

As the national election of 1800 approached, the leaders of both parties recognized that so crucial a matter as the selection of the president of the United States no longer could be entrusted, as the Founding Fathers had entrusted it, to the uncontrolled vagaries of the Electoral College. Accordingly, each party's congressional caucus selected a national "ticket" for 1800—Jefferson and Aaron Burr for the Republicans, and John Adams and Charles Cotesworth Pinckney for the Federalists. Moreover, the leaders of both parties in the states made it clear that members of the Electoral College should be chosen not because they would exercise good judgment but because they could be counted on to vote for the Jefferson-Burr ticket or the Adams-Pinckney ticket. South Carolina was typical: the Republican members of the legislature caucused and named a committee to prepare a list of electors. Each prospective elector then was interviewed to make sure of his loyalty to Jefferson and Burr, the persons chosen became the Republican slate of electors, and the legislature chose the entire slate over the Federalist competition.[14]

Many history books portray the election of 1800 mainly in terms of the tie in the Electoral College, the patriotism of Hamilton in persuading Federalist electors to vote for Jefferson over Burr, and the subsequent adoption of the Twelfth Amendment requiring the electors to cast separate ballots for president and vice-president. But the historians and political scientists who are more concerned with the constitutional system as defined here believe that the election of 1800 was one of the most important in our history because it marked the advent of "Article VIII" rather than because it led to the Twelfth Amendment. Many, indeed, regard it as one of the great milestones in the history not only of the United States but also of democratic development everywhere. For it was, they point out, "the first election in modern history which, by popular decision, resulted in the quiet and peaceful transition of national power from the hands of one of two embattled parties to another."[15]

The Final Stage

The happy outcome of 1800 was by no means as inevitable as it may seem to us after nearly two centuries of seeing losing parties peacefully accept the legitimacy of the winners, with the one terrible exception of the election of 1860. We would do well to remember, however, that many leaders and followers of each party at the time deeply believed that the other party was a subversive conspiracy whose victory might well plunge the nation into atheism and bankruptcy, or into a monarchy ruled by the plutocrats of New England. Yet, even though most of the Federalist losers loathed and feared Jefferson and his minions, they did not mount an armed rebellion against him. One reason was certainly the fact that many of them saw the election as only a temporary setback; they believed that the Republicans would mismanage affairs, the people would soon come to their senses, and the Federalists would return to power in 1802 or 1804. A more enduring reason, though, was the nation's slow movement into the fifth and final stage of party development: the general acceptance of the idea that competition for power between two well-organized political parties is an acceptable, even desirable, way to realize the principle that the only legitimate basis for government is the consent of the governed.

Let us remember that, during stage four of the development of American political parties, most Federalists and Republicans did not see the opposing party as an organization very much like themselves, which differed with them only on questions of what measures would best promote the national interest sought by all members of both parties. Rather, the adherents of each party saw the other as antithetical to, and subversive of, the basic principles of the Republic itself. It was this view that, in the late 1790s, induced the Federalist Congress to pass the Alien and Sedition acts, making it a penal offense to form a combination to criticize the government or its leading officers. It was the same view that induced the Republicans to respond by enacting the Virginia and Kentucky resolutions declaring the Federalist acts unconstitutional and, in effect, refusing to obey them.

As Seymour Martin Lipset points out, these attitudes toward organized political opposition remain alive and well in many of the new nations of the twentieth century, and for much the same reasons. In his words:

> The various efforts by both Federalists and Democratic-Republicans to repress the rights of their opponents clearly indicate that in many ways our early political officials resembled those heads of new states in the twentieth century who view criticism of themselves as tantamount to an attack on the nation itself. Such behavior characterizes leaders of polities in which the concept of democratic succession to office has not been institutionalized....To accept criticism as proper requires the prior acceptance of the view that opposition and succession are normal, and that men may be loyal to the policy and yet disapprove of the particular set of incumbents. This view does not come easily to men who have themselves created a polity, and cannot, therefore, conceive of it functioning properly without them or in ways other than they think best.[16]

Hofstadters's magisterial study of Americans' eventual acceptance of organized party competition details Lipset's thesis. He points out that, even though most of the political leaders of the 1780s became deeply involved in the emerging party politics of the Republic's first thirty years, most of them had grave reservations about its legitimacy, although some, notably Madison and Jefferson, occasionally suggested that there was potential for good as well as danger in party competition.[17] Most of them believed that that happy day finally had arrived after the War of 1812, when the Federalist party disintegrated and almost everyone, leaders and followers alike, became Republicans. James Monroe, for example, believed that his nearly unanimous reelection in 1820 signaled the end of party discord, and indeed some historians have dubbed the era of one-party rule from 1816 to 1828 as "the era of good feelings."

Few eras have been so mislabeled. After the collapse of the Federalists, the often bitter but well-structured interparty competition of the preceding twenty years was replaced by the equally bitter but far more chaotic intraparty factional competition of the mid-1820s. But, as Hofstadter points out, the generation of the Framers was being replaced by a new generation of leaders typified by the members of the Albany Regency, such as Governor and Senator William L. Marcy, Governor and Senator Enos T. Throop, and, above all, Vice-president and President Martin Van Buren.

The new leaders differed from the old in two critical respects. First, they had not created a new constitutional order but had grown up in and took for granted the order created and confirmed by the

Framers. Accordingly, they did not regard criticisms of themselves and their policies as treason, or their critics as enemies of the Constitution and the nation. Rivals in business, yes; subversives, no. Second, they saw the so-called era of good feelings not as the final triumph of national unity but as the degeneration of the original party system's conflict over great principles into the confused and petty factional squabbles that characterized the one-party politics of the 1820s.

Whatever their motives, the new leaders turned the one-party factionalism of the 1820s into the nation's "second-party system"— the two-party conflict between the Democrats of Van Buren and Andrew Jackson and the Whigs of Henry Clay and Daniel Webster.[18] In 1831 and 1832 the new parties held the first national delegate conventions ever for the purpose of nominating presidential candidates and writing national platforms, and in 1840 they established national committees to conduct party affairs between presidential elections.

Most important, the new generation of political leaders proudly declared their dedication to the proposition that open competition over offices and policies between two well-defined, well-organized, and permanent political parties is the best way—perhaps the only way—to operate a government that will be both responsive to the people's wishes and accountable to them for its successes and failures. As Governor Throop put it in 1829:

> Those party divisions which are based upon conflicting opinions in regard to the constitution of the government, or the measures of the administration of it, interest every citizen, and tend...to reduce the many shades of opinion into two opposing parties....Organized parties watch and scan each other's doings, the public mind is instructed by ample discussions of public measures, and acts of violence are restrained by the convictions of the people, that the prevailing measures are the results of enlightened reason.[19]

When most Americans came to believe that, as they did in the 1830s and 1840s, the first section of the Constitution's "Article VIII" was completed, and the world's first large-scale modern democracy had accomplished one of its most important changes. Today, as in 1863, it remains to be seen whether a system "so conceived and so dedicated can long endure." But there is no doubt that for nearly two centuries the competition between our two great political parties has been an integral part of government by the people, as organized in our constitutional system.

NOTES

[1]Walter Bagehot, *The English Constitution* (1867), World Classics Edition (London, 1952), 1.

[2]This apt phrase is the title of Chap. 2 of Richard Hofstadter, *The Idea of a Party System* (Berkeley, 1970). In this section I have relied heavily on Hofstadter's ideas and data and on the analysis in William Nisbet Chambers, *Political Parties in a New Nation: The American Experience, 1776–1809* (New York, 1963). See also Noble E. Cunningham, Jr., ed., *The Making of the American Party System, 1789 to 1809* (Englewood Cliffs, NJ, 1965); Edgar E. Robinson, *The Evolution of American Political Parties* (New York, 1924); and Seymour Martin Lipset, *The First New Nation* (New York, 1963).

[3]For a more detailed description of the general developmental pattern of democratic parties, see Austin Ranney and Willmoore Kendall, *Democracy and the American Party System* (1956; reprint, Westport, 1974), chap. 5.

[4]Quoted in Hofstadter, *The Idea of a Party System*, 97.

[5]James Madison, in Clinton Rossiter, ed., *The Federalist Papers* (New York, 1961), No. 10, 77.

[6]Ibid., 78.

[7]Ibid., 81.

[8]Ibid., 83.

[9]No. 47 in ibid., 301.

[10]No. 51 in ibid., 324.

[11]Written in a letter to the committee in charge of the celebration of the centennial of the Constitution on July 20, 1887.

[12]Hofstadter, *The Idea of a Party System*, 95.

[13]Chambers, *Political Parties in a New Nation*, 44–45.

[14]Ibid., 157–58.

[15]Hofstadter, *The Idea of a Party System*, 128.

[16]Lipset, *The First New Nation*, 43–44.

[17]See, for example, Hofstadter's collection of antiparty and proparty statements by both leaders: *The Idea of a Party System*, 81–83, 114–16, 204–6.

[18]The most complete account of the emergence of the new two-party politics is Richard P. McCormick, *The Second American Party System: Party Formation in the Jacksonian Era* (Chapel Hill, 1966). See also McCormick, "Political Development and the Second Party System," in William Nisbet Chambers and Walter Dean Burnham, eds., *The American Party Systems: Stages of Political Development* (New York, 1967), 90–116.

[19]Quoted in Hofstadter, *The Idea of a Party System*, 251. Hofstadter believed that the most complete statement of the radical new doctrine—that organized two-party competition is a good thing—is Martin Van Buren's book, *Inquiry into the Origins and Course of Political Parties in the United States*, edited by his sons and published posthumously in 1867 by Hurd & Houghton in New York.

Commentary to Austin Ranney

Daniel A. Mazmanian

Professor Ranney has taken his charge quite seriously and literally. He has provided an excellent summary of the rapid rise in the legitimacy and culturally accepted functions of political groups, factions, and parties during the crucial formative years of our nation.

Although I might argue with Professor Ranney over just how strong was the antiparty sentiment of a Washington, or a Jefferson, or a Monroe and their compatriots, or just how compelling the attraction of organized groups, factions, and electoral parties may have been at any given juncture in the early decades of the nation, I could not agree more with his basic message and conclusion: that almost instantly the group, the faction, the party moved center stage in the political and electoral life of the young Republic. Indeed, political parties became the cornerstone of our system of representative government. As Professor Ranney states in his closing remarks, moreover, political parties have remained central to our political process through the past two hundred years.

Still, I fear that, in stopping here and saying no more, we fail to take full advantage of our forum. It is not only a celebration of the new national charter on its 200th birthday, but also a time for taking stock and looking ahead. In the past two decades, according to many keen observers, political parties have undergone as rapid and profound an evolution as in the early moments referred to by Professor Ranney. Yet this evolution has been characterized by a diminution of the proper and necessary functioning of political parties as the central mobilizing, integrating, educating, and politically socializing institutions in our democratic society. What I mean by this is quite simple, and indeed it is intimately linked to the long and distinguished professional life of Professor Ranney, spanning his thoughts and writings from at least the early 1950s.

The issue is that, even in the late eighteenth century, it was evident to some of the most profound political minds of the day that representative government, to be true to those represented, necessitated cooperation among large numbers of persons within enduring, programmatic, and policy-oriented political parties. In the words of one of the most remembered Englishmen of the late eighteenth century, Edmund Burke:

> Whilst men are linked together, they easily and speedily communicate the alarm of any evil design. They are enabled to fathom it with common counsel, and to oppose it with united strength. Whereas, when they lie dispersed, without concern, order, or discipline, communication is uncertain, counsel difficult, and resistance impracticable.... When bad men combine, the good must associate; else they will fall, one by one, an unpitied sacrifice in a contemptible struggle. *(Thoughts on the Cause of the Present Discontents)*

This has not necessarily been the dominant view among the public at large in the United States, but its compelling logic attracted scholars from Woodrow Wilson and A. Lawrence Lowell at the turn of the nineteenth century down through E. E. Schattschneider and Willmoore Kendall. It was Professor Ranney, moreover, in 1962, who wrote *The Doctrine of Responsible Party Government,* a persuasive book on the importance of the kinds of parties that could aggregate views across a diverse population, build enduring social and political coalitions, teach the arts of compromise and consensus building to their members, and serve as the great mediating institutions in our democracy.

Admittedly, today the issue is rarely joined as to whether or not to have responsible parties, so much as whether parties serve even a semblance of the role of clarifying issues, aggregating interests, and helping to translate broad majority views into well-thought-out and formulated public policies. Our attention is drawn, as recent titles suggest, to *The Current Crisis in American Politics* (Walter Dean Burnham) and *American Parties in Decline* (William Crotty and Gary Jacobson). Similarly, our focus is on the rise of special interests, extreme factions, and the Goliaths of today's electoral arena— political action committees. Ironically, if we look closely at why contemporary analysts bemoan the sorry state of our party system, it is precisely because it has become riddled with the kind of factionalized, acrimonious, self-seeking, self-righteous, and disparate interests so assuredly promised us by Madison in *The Federalist* No. 10 and viewed by the Founders as just the right antidote to tyrannical government.

In short, at least a good case can be made that the recent past, and likely near-term future, has brought us full circle to the desired state of group conflict so championed as the Madisonian ideal: many different factions, organized to pursue their own narrow interests on an ad hoc basis, blocking one another in the system of checks and balances so characteristic of the American political arena, although coming together for periodic "coalitions of convenience." The reasons for this are many, going back as far as the replacement of patronage systems once controlled by parties from the federal down to the lowest level of public services beginning in the 1880s. Also, no longer do political parties greet and introduce into American politics and culture large masses of immigrants, which they did so well in the late nineteenth and early twentieth century. Furthermore, parties no longer have a monopoly in serving office seekers as their eyes and ears into the electorate. Today, professional pollsters and public relations and mass media experts largely perform these functions. Meanwhile, into the void left by parties have stepped the many diverse special interests with their own means of reaching out to the voters, their own brand of political message, and their own sense of appropriate public policy, just as envisioned in "Article VIII."

This turn of events is being taken by many pundits as signaling the death knell of the kind of responsible party government Professor Ranney pointed us to in his 1962 book: that is, a party system that not only serves the politically active, rich, and well-to-do but also one in which nationally representative parties mobilize and serve those ever struggling to surmount the economic, educational, racial, ethnic, religious, and personal barriers confronting them in the political arena of our grand and illustrious Republic.

In this sense, then, we have come full circle from birth to 200th birthday, starting with a system of factions and back again. I have serious reservations about whether this is a development worthy of praise and celebration. Rather, we could use this celebration of two hundred years of governance under the Constitution not only to take a retrospective look at political parties, but also to pursue a fundamental reassessment of their necessary and potential role in a democratic society, and to consider what new "articles" to the Constitution might be needed to ensure that this role is fulfilled.

RECOMMENDED READING

Crotty, William. *Party Reform*. New York, 1983.
Price, David E. *Bringing Back the Parties*. Washington, DC, 1984.
Ranney, Austin. *The Doctrine of Responsible Party Government*. Urbana, 1962.
Rose, Richard. *Do Parties Make a Difference?* Chatham, NJ, 1984.

Scott, Ruth K., and Ronald J. Hrebenar. *Parties in Crisis: Party Politics in America.* New York, 1984.
Sundquist, James L. *Dynamics of the Party System: Alignment and Realignment of Political Parties in the United States.* Rev. ed. Washington, DC, 1983.

The Right to Vote: Constitutional Principles and Contemporary Ramifications

C. Lani Guinier

> If liberty and equality, as is thought by some,
> are chiefly to be found in democracy, they will
> be best attained when all persons alike share
> in the government to the utmost.
> —Aristotle *Politics* 4.4

The occasion of the bicentennial of the Constitution of the United States evokes consideration of the extent to which the Constitution compels adherence to this principle. Specifically, two hundred years after the founding of our Republic, the constitutional debate still rages over allocations of political power, the nature of political representation, the meaning of political equality, and the significance of political rights, including the right to vote. Until blacks and other minorities are fully engaged in the mainstream of our political system, our two-hundred-year experiment with Aristotle's democratic federation will have failed.

To civil rights advocates in the twentieth century, political emancipation always has been crucial.[1] "Give us our ballot," Charles Evers, recently discharged from the armed services, told a Mississippi registrar in 1946. Physically barred from enrolling at the Decatur courthouse, Evers nevertheless concluded that the way local whites "guarded that ballot box, they let us know there was something mighty good in voting."[2] A potent weapon of political empowerment and an important measure of human dignity, the right to vote was fundamental to preserve all rights.

The decision to address the political exclusion and isolation of blacks was first made by Congress in 1870, with the passage of the Fifteenth Amendment, and reaffirmed as recently as 1982 when it extended and strengthened the Voting Rights Act of 1965. But the crippling lack of enforcement of these laws by the present administration and the tortured efforts of many local functionaries to evade their reach belie a commitment to full political participation. As the U.S. Commission on Civil Rights warned eighteen years ago, "The right to vote will not be realized fully unless the burden of taking affirmative action to encourage [its exercise] is shared by the Federal Government."[3] Yet, in an apocryphal reversal of a three-decade bipartisan national consensus, the federal government is realigning itself with local officials who are obstructing and chilling the exercise of the franchise. When combined with the idiosyncratic, unduly technical, balkanized, and burdensome features of contemporary electoral participation, these attacks on the franchise, although relatively invisible to most, threaten the bedrock of our constitutional democracy. On the other hand, if the Fifteenth Amendment and the Voting Rights Act were vigorously enforced, the promise of "all persons alike sharing in government to the utmost" would be fulfilled to the benefit not only of blacks but also of everyone.

Constitutional Principles

The right to vote has been called the "crown jewel of American liberties,"[4] the "cherished right of people in a country like ours,"[5] and the "inalienable right"[6] of each and every citizen. The extravagant contemporary rhetoric certainly implies the existence of a fundamental constitutional right, as drafted in 1787, but the Constitution did not confer the right of suffrage to citizens of the United States.[7] Indeed, the Framers did not provide a right of suffrage to anyone. Control of the qualifications of voters was vested in the states.[8] When our nation began, white men without property were denied the right to vote.[9] Women, blacks, and Indians also were not "considered qualified to participate in the republican experiment."[10]

Even after passage of the Fourteenth[11] and Fifteenth[12] Amendments, the Constitution did not establish the franchise unequivocally as a privilege or immunity of citizenship. Written in the negative as a prohibition of denial of the franchise on the basis of race, the Fifteenth Amendment simply furnished a guarantee that classes of voters created by the states could not be silhouetted by explicitly racial criteria.[13] Operating as it did through the states and not directly upon the citizen, the Fifteenth Amendment tolerated literacy tests,[14] poll taxes,[15] white primaries,[16] and onerous systems of personal registration.[17] Though enacted in response to a demand for national protection against abuses of state power, the proscriptive rather than prescriptive wording of the Fifteenth Amendment ultimately left the states free to evade its reach as long as the barriers they devised against blacks voting were not overtly racial. Until the 1965 Voting Rights Act, the language of the amendment proved inadequate for protecting black suffrage.[18]

Initially, immediately after its passage, democratic reforms temporarily swept the South. The apparatus of federal authority was deployed to ensure that the suffrage was granted to blacks and whites on the same basis.[19] Moreover, federally appointed registrars traversed the countryside by every form of mid-nineteenth-century conveyance, including rowboats and wagons,[20] to enroll new voters. Despite war-related white disqualifications, in Mississippi, for example, approximately 80 percent of all eligible voters were registered.[21] However, once federal troops were removed pursuant to the Hayes-Tilden Compromise of 1877, the federal effort to enfranchise blacks entered a dormant state that lasted through the first half of the next century. With its demise, the establishment of suffrage requirements devolved once again to the states, which quickly instituted restrictive registration procedures to disenfranchise blacks and some poor whites. For example, in 1896, 164,088 white voters and 130,344 black voters were registered in Louisiana. In 1904, subsequent to passage of new registration requirements, white registration fell to 106,360, and black registrants numbered only 1,718.[22]

The institution of these turn-of-the-century voter registration statutes depressed voter participation nationwide.[23] The national government reentered the political thicket in the 1950s and 1960s to redeem the promise of representative government, but, despite passage of successive constitutional amendments expanding suffrage to women[24] and outlawing the poll tax in federal elections,[25] our democratic principles have coexisted uneasily with practical impediments to voting. Even after the Supreme Court forcefully endorsed an affirmative constitutional right of each individual to vote,[26] enfranchisement of blacks occurred episodically and only after a national crisis precipitated in 1965 a significant departure from past policies. The Voting Rights Act of that year extended the suffrage of southern blacks only by readjusting the allocation of power within the federal system.[27] One hundred years after the end of the Civil War, federal registrars again functioned in the South as they had during Reconstruction.[28] The federal government finally reclaimed the franchise from southern whites, who had been aided in perpetuating discrimination by a national constitution which ceded to state prerogative the control of voter qualifications.

Still, twentieth-century Americans persevere in their ambivalence toward the franchise as the subject of national regulation. Even as the Constitution symbolically recognized the political rights of illiterates,[29] transients,[30] and indeed the homeless,[31] election regulations and voter qualifications still are governed by a hodgepodge of state laws and ultimately are entrusted to local authorities, whose discretionary practices remain arbitrary,[32] restrictive,[33] and discriminatory.[34] These state-erected barriers to registration continue to discourage citizens, particularly blacks, from exercising their right to vote.

Having mounted the constitutional summit as an individual right, the franchise is still viewed by many as a privilege which the individual voter must earn.[35] Moreover, constitutional principles remain ambiguous as to whether the franchise is a group right whose free, unencumbered, and undiluted exercise is the essence of democratic society. While finally embracing the right to vote as an individual right, the one-person-one-vote principle of *Reynolds v. Sims*[36] and its progeny may actually accord a higher standard of constitutional protection of majority rule than minority group voting rights.[37] Sophisticated schemes of discounting the vote to racial minorities, for example, have been upheld as constitutional[38] in the absence of proof that their discriminatory effects were intentional.[39]

It was precisely to reach dilution of minority group voting strength that might evade protection under the exacting constitutional intent test that Congress in 1982 amended Section 2 of the Voting Rights Act. As amended, Section 2 recognizes the group nature of voting rights and guarantees to minorities the "opportunity ...to elect candidates of their choice."[40] By rejecting the constitutionally imposed requirement that racial vote dilution claims be given asylum only from intentionally discriminatory state action,[41] Congress attempted to legislate a new results-oriented standard of political equality warranting "more exacting judicial protection."[42] For the first time since 1787, blacks and other minorities were promised even more than a badge of citizenship and dignity. The foundation stone for political action, for seeking redress from and representation in government at local, state, and federal levels, finally had been laid.

Contemporary Ramifications

Twenty-two years after congressional action to enforce the Fourteenth and Fifteenth Amendments through enactment of the Voting Rights Act,[43] blacks still are not elected to positions of power in this society in numbers reflecting their presence in the population. There are no blacks in the U.S. Senate, no black congressional representatives from states in which they comprise more than 25 percent of the population, no black governors, and only a handful of blacks elected to state judicial office.[44] Beyond the numbers, the issues of concern to the black community are not generally debated in the councils of government, except in symbolic and desultory ways. Even where blacks are elected to local or state office, the legacy of racism inhibits the building of coalitions and the establishing of bases of power that extend into the larger society. Professor Owen Fiss sees this severely limited political power as deriving from three different yet interrelated sources:

> One source of weakness is their numbers, the fact that they are a numerical minority; the second is their economic status, their position as the perpetual underclass, and the third is that as a "discrete and insular" minority, they are the object of "prejudice"—that is, the subject of fear, hatred, and distaste that make it particularly difficult for them to form coalitions with others (such as the white poor) and that make it advantageous for the dominant political parties to hurt them—to use them as a scapegoat.[45]

Given the scope of interconnected problems identified by Professor Fiss and others, voting rights are by definition limited. We cannot, simply by filing lawsuits or enacting legislation, change the numerical or economic status of blacks in this society, nor can we expect to eliminate racial polarization by court decree. But we can challenge the sophisticated, as well as the simple-minded, barriers to black representation, with the hope that by empowering blacks we are providing the black community with tools to make more far-reaching gains.[46]

We start with the basic truism that representative democracy rests on the consent of the governed. Two major questions test the legitimacy of this basic democratic assumption for blacks: the nature of the representation and the extent of consent. Pursuant to Section 2 of the Voting Rights Act as amended in 1982, current voting rights litigation by the NAACP Legal Defense Fund and other advocacy groups reflects the impact of these broad themes on the black community.

Vote Dilution (Representation Cases)

The first issue, the nature of representation, questions whether those elected advocate the interests of the black community; whether the community, if it chooses, can elect persons who typify its interests; or whether black voters can hold their representatives electorally accountable. The aim of "representation" cases is to prove that those whom the black community perceives as best representing its interests do not get elected in numbers that fairly reflect the percentage of blacks in the population. Although the issue is not simply the number of blacks elected to office in the jurisdiction, our lawsuits do assume a value in electing black office holders. Blacks in positions of responsibility within the local governing boards serve as role models; they have a salutary effect on the type of language used and the issues considered within the councils of government; they give blacks access to the levers of government (even blacks living outside their district campaign for them, bring their problems to them, and consider them "representative"); and, finally, they are in a position to advocate vigorously the interests of those who elected them.

The thrust of our representation cases is directed at vote dilution schemes in communities where blacks, although a sizable voting minority, exercise little or no political leverage. Such schemes minimize the voting strength of black voters so that those who are elected do not represent the interests of the black community and are not accountable to the community for reelection. Proving a vote dilution case involves demonstrating the existence of a geographically identifiable black community with common interests, different from those of the white majority, where voting is polarized on racial lines to the extent that candidates supported by the minority community do not get elected over a period of time or in the numbers one would expect. At-large elections,[47] majority vote run-off requirements,[48] staggered terms,[49] and gerrymandered districts[50] are examples of the structural barriers that we challenge in our representation cases.

Access to Ballot (Registration Litigation)

The United States now ranks next to last among Western democracies in voter participation. Throughout most of the twentieth century the overwhelmingly dominant party in the United States has been the "party of the nonvoters."[51] In the 1980 election, for example, of our voting-age population only 52.6 percent voted for president; 77 million Americans stayed home. In 1982 only 37.7 percent voted for members of Congress.[52] Yet studies, such as "Voting for Democracy" produced by the Harvard/ABC Symposium in 1983, consistently show that if people are registered then they vote in overwhelming numbers.[53] Blacks and Hispanics, in the past, have had a mediocre record of participation in the electoral process. However, according to the symposium figures, of those registered in 1980, 84.7 percent of the blacks and 83.3 percent of the Hispanics turned out to vote in the presidential race.

By election day most Americans would like to vote, but many, especially minorities, are not registered because the United States permits a variety of state-erected barriers to simple and convenient registration. Most voter registration requirements in the United States were enacted in the late 1800s to exclude blacks in the South and new immigrants in the North from voting.[54] Although such requirements have been rationalized by the need to prevent voter fraud, most election fraud occurs in voting, not in registration, and is typically committed by election officials, not private individuals.[55] Whatever their arguable conceptual justification, in practice these requirements serve primarily to reduce voter participation among all citizens in the United States and especially among minorities and poor people.

In a number of states we have filed lawsuits challenging restrictive registration laws and procedures. Here, again, we are using the Constitution and the 1965 Voting Rights Act, as amended in 1982.[56] These cases contend that overt barriers still exist to keep blacks from registering and voting "their consent." By placing the responsibility for getting on the voting rolls upon the shoulders of the individual voters and by making it difficult for those without cars, telephones, or a tradition of political participation to register, incumbent white politicians effectively control the electorate to preserve the status quo. For example, many rural counties have only one place to register—closed weekends, evenings, and at lunch. Other counties refuse to appoint blacks as volunteer deputy registrars who could go door to door to register blacks.

Large numbers of blacks are not registered and thus are outside the political process. The number of unregistered blacks ranges from just under 1 million in New York to close to 500,000 in Georgia. We are challenging the system of registration to try to get the states to assume more of the responsibility for compiling voting lists and to act more affirmatively to get blacks on those lists. The theory behind affirmative outreach to make registration accessible to the black community is that the effects of historic voting discrimination still linger both in terms of a present gap between black and white registration rates and a depressed socioeconomic status that makes inconvenient registration especially burdensome for blacks. Although voting is hailed as the "crown jewel of American liberties," registration procedures, with their local idiosyncrasies, all have built-in costs—informational, psychological, logistical, and sociological. These costs are more burdensome to black and other minority citizens, a disproportionate number of whom are poor and many of whom live most of their adult lives in atmospheres officially and pervasively hostile to their exercise of the franchise. Although the important work of registering and educating new voters must proceed, as we see it, our long-term opportunity lies in changing how Americans approach the concept and implement the requirements of pre-voting registration procedures.

The federal and state governments have succeeded in convincing us that it is our burden to get names on the voter rolls. Most other democratic governments assume the responsibility, both financial and administrative, of canvassing eligible voters to register them.[57] Yet, here in the United States, volunteers and private agencies willingly perform this governmental function.

Short of full government responsibility of universal suffrage, there are several potential short-term reforms, including mandatory appointment of black deputy registrars, mail registration with forms disseminated via post office change-of-address forms or utility service connections, and public agency registration at motor vehicle bureaus, unemployment offices, and welfare departments. No system short of door-to-door canvassing by government employees or expense-paid volunteers will achieve dramatic increases in black participation, but each of the above possibilities represents an improvement on present procedures, particularly in the South. A combination of two or three of the proposed methods would be most effective, although still not perfect. The real advantage is that each reform makes the next reform easier, while creating a climate for public affirmation of the ultimate goal of greater government registration initiatives.[58] Moreover, as the responsibility for registration gradually is returned to state and local governments, volunteers and civil rights groups will have more resources, time, and energy to address the even more fundamental and troublesome problem of moving the black community beyond the symbolic act of voting to full-fledged political participation, decision making, and electoral accountability.

What is still needed is to put the registration issue front and center on the national agenda. What better occasion than the Bicentennial to spotlight the enormous number of unregistered voters? The pressure should be on the county registrars, secretaries of state, members of Congress, and on the state and national parties to demonstrate their commitment both to constitutional principles and to enforcing the Voting Rights Act, to make registration simple and accessible for all eligible citizens. Finally, the Department of Justice, which has authority to appoint federal examiners under Section 6(b) of the Act, should use that authority to supplement the inaction of county registrars in those states covered by Section 5.

Conclusion

Expanding the base of political participation is essential to the continued vitality of our democratic experiment. Blacks, Hispanics, and poor people should enjoy not only the constitutionally affirmed right to cast a ballot but also the right to cast a meaningful ballot, the right to elect representatives of their choice—representatives who advocate their interests and are accountable electorally to them. Without such rights, political participation can be futile, our constitutional principles bereft.

The right to vote should be interpreted broadly as the right of meaningful access to the political process, the right to have one's voice heard in the councils of government rather than interpreted narrowly as a privilege of registration and access to the ballot box, the burden of whose exercise is carried by the individual, unassisted and unleavened by the federal government.

This point was identified in an op-ed piece in the *New York Times* entitled, "The Vote Has a Moat," describing current passive voter registration systems:

> [T]he notion has taken hold that voting is some sort of "privilege" for which the citizen has to suffer some inconvenience, if not actually put up a fight against the bureaucrats. That is the sort of situation that could produce apathy where none was to be found before. The nation needs to change its political attitudes about voting, to come around to the view, general in other democracies, that it is part of government's job to make it as easy as possible for every citizen to vote. While government may not require people to vote, it ought actively to be soliciting them to participate. If government would undertake to register every eligible person, we might still

find voters apathetic on Election Day. On the other hand, we might find our democracy as healthy as any other.[59]

The choice is not acquiescence by the "silent minorities" in nonparticipatory, nonrepresentative ways of governing. We need to shape our electorate so that silent minorities become consensual partners.[60] But consent alone is not enough. Support and legitimacy for our constitutional system also depend on increased political participation in all phases of decision making, not just in the polling place.

More political participation by blacks and other minorities does not mean less participation by others. Politics is not a zero-sum game.[61] Indeed, everyone gains more freedom and more equality when more people participate effectively. As Thomas Jefferson said, "In democracy, agreement is not essential, but participation is."

NOTES

[1]Although Booker T. Washington reportedly accepted the idea of restricted suffrage for both races, Dr. Martin Luther King, Jr., called the right to vote the number-one civil right. Other black leaders, inspired by W. E. B. Du Bois and the NAACP, have been committed to extending the franchise through litigation, nonviolent protest, and dramatic voter registration campaigns. Steven F. Lawson, *Black Ballots: Voting Rights in the South* (New York, 1976), 13–14.

[2]Charles Evers, *Evers* (New York, 1971), 92–96.

[3]U.S. Commission on Civil Rights, *Political Participation* (Washington, DC, 1968), 186.

[4]Presidential Signing Statement, 42 U.S.C. §1973 (1982).

[5]*Louisiana v. United States*, 380 U.S. 145, 153 (1965).

[6]*Reynolds v. Sims*, 377 U.S. 533, 565 (1964).

[7]*Minor v. Happersett*, 88 U.S. 162 (1874).

[8]U.S. Const. art. I, §2, cl. 1. See *Minor v. Happersett*, 88 U.S. at 172–73, listing the qualifications for voting applicable in the states when the Constitution was adopted. In no state were all citizens permitted to vote.

[9]See *Harper v. Virginia Board of Elections*, 383 U.S. 663, 675 (1966) (Black, J. dissenting).

[10]Lawson, *Black Ballots*, 11.

[11]Section 1 of the Fourteenth Amendment provides: "All persons born or naturalized in the United States, and subject to the jurisdiction thereof, are citizens of the United States and of the State wherein they reside. No State shall make or enforce any law which shall abridge the privileges or immunities of citizens of the United States; nor shall any State deprive any person of life, liberty, or property, without due process of law; nor deny to

any person within its jurisdiction the equal protection of the laws." Section 2 of the Fourteenth Amendment dealt backhandedly with the franchise by reducing proportionately a state's representation in Congress if any adult males were disenfranchised.

[12]The Fifteenth Amendment provides: "Section 1. The right of citizens of the United States to vote shall not be denied or abridged by the United States or by any State on account of race, color, or previous condition of servitude. Section 2. Congress shall have power to enforce this article by appropriate legislation."

[13]*United States v. Cruikshank*, 92 U.S. 542 (1876); *United States v. Reese*, 92 U.S. 214 (1876). It was only when Congress exercised its authority to pass appropriate legislation by enacting the Enforcement Act in 1870, amended in 1871 and finally augmented by enforcement machinery beginning in 1957, that an affirmative guarantee of the right to vote in all national and state elections became part of our jurisprudence. See 42 U.S.C. §1971(a) (1) (1970).

[14]*Lassiter v. Northampton County Board of Elections*, 360 U.S. 45 (1959).

[15]*Breedlove v. Suttles*, 302 U.S. 277 (1937).

[16]*Grovey v. Townsend*, 295 U.S. 45 (1935).

[17]Enacted by many states in the late nineteenth century, voter registration laws reduced electoral turnout, particularly among blacks in the South and among poor, less educated whites nationwide. Previously, all qualified citizens were able to vote without first registering. In the words of J. Morgan Kousser, "By lengthening residency requirements, by requiring periodic voter registration at centrally located places during working hours and presentation of registration receipts at the polls (which burdened lower-class voters who were not accustomed, in those prebureaucratic days, to keeping records), by demanding copiously detailed information,...by allowing registration boards sufficient discretion to enable them to pad or unfairly purge the rolls, by not guaranteeing equal party representation on such boards, and by permitting widespread challenges to voters at the polls, nineteenth-century Southern Democrats could keep the black vote under control." "The Undermining of the First Reconstruction: Lessons for the Second," in C. Davidson, ed., *Minority Vote Dilution* (Washington, DC, 1984), 33.

[18]Not only did the proscriptive language of the amendment limit its effectiveness but also subsequent Supreme Court interpretations encouraged "the belief that it is possible, through state enactments, to defeat the beneficent purpose which the people of the United States had in view when they adopted the [Fourteenth and Fifteenth] Amendments to the Constitution." *Plessy v. Ferguson*, 163 U.S. 537, 560 (1896) (Harlan, J. dissenting).

[19]Michael Perman, *Reunion without Compromise: The South and Reconstruction, 1865–1868* (Cambridge, England, 1973), 68–81; Kenneth Stampp, *The Era of Reconstruction, 1865–1877* (New York, 1965).

[20]W. C. Harris, *The Day of the Carpetbagger: Republican Reconstruction in Mississippi* (Baton Rouge, 1979), 67–74.

[21] Report by Dr. Steven Hahn, "Historical Circumstances and Purposes Involved in the Adoption of Dual Registration and the Abolition of Satellite Registration by the State of Mississippi," to be filed in U.S. District Court, N.D. Miss., *PUSH v. Allain*, No. D.C. 84-35-wk-0 (February 1986), 7.

[22] "Access to Voter Registration," 9 Harvard Civil Rights-Civil Liberties Law Review 482, 486 (1974).

[23] Until the late nineteenth century, all qualified citizens were able to vote without first registering. 9 Harvard Civil Rights-Civil Liberties Law Review at 482.

[24] Nineteenth Amendment.

[25] Twenty-fourth Amendment.

[26] It was in the reapportionment decisions of the 1960s that the Court announced the new constitutional right to vote as one person, one vote. These decisions have been variously criticized as reflecting the personal commitment of members of the Court to principles of majority rule, freezing one theory of political thought into the Constitution and creating an impending conflict between the individual constitutional right of voters within population majorities to representational control of elected officials and the group right of minority voters to special constitutional protection. See, for example, "At-Large Elections and One Person, One Vote," Blacksher and Menefee, in Davidson, *Minority Vote Dilution.*

[27] When President Lyndon Johnson signed the 1965 Voting Rights Act, a national civil rights leader proclaimed it a "milestone and every bit as momentous and significant...as the Emancipation Proclamation or the 1954 Supreme Court decision" in *Brown v. School Board of Topeka.* John L. Lewis, quoted by Lawson, *Black Ballots,* 321.

[28] Lawson, *Black Ballots,* 340.

[29] *Oregon v. Mitchell,* 400 U.S. 112 (1970).

[30] *Dunn v. Blumstein,* 405 U.S. 330 (1972); see also *City of Phoenix v. Kolodyieski,* 399 U.S. 204 (1970); *Cipriano v. City of Houma,* 395 U.S. 701 (1969); *Kramer v. Union Free School District,* 395 U.S. 621 (1969).

[31] See generally Dollin, "Voting Rights of the Homeless," 14 Stetson L. Rev. (1985), cited in Gelfand, "Voting Rights and the Democratic Process: Ongoing Struggles and Continuing Questions," 17 Urban Lawyer 333, 334 n.8 (1985).

[32] See, for example, *NAACP, DeKalb County v. Georgia,* 494 F. Supp. 668, 672 (N.D. Ga. 1980) (policy of county board of registrars erratic).

[33] *Project Vote! v. Ohio Bureau of Employment Services,* 578 F. Supp. 7 (S.D. Ohio 1982).

[34] See, for example, *Rhode Island Minority Caucus, Inc. v. Baronian,* 590 F.2d 372 (1st Cir. 1979); *Beare v. Briscoe,* 498 F.2d 244 (5th Cir. 1974), affirming *Beare v. Smith,* 321 F. Supp. 1100 (S.D. Tex. 1971).

[35] According to Walter Dean Burnham, personal registration is accepted because it fits well into the "underlying hegemonic ideology" of individualism. Voting is seen as a privilege which the individual, by registering, proves he is qualified to exercise. Although this approach frames

voting as a test and not a right of citizenship, its antidemocratic consequences have historically been borne, in part, to avoid accepting the presence of "large numbers of blacks in the active electorate." "The Appearance
and Disappearance of the American Voter," Thomas Ferguson and Joel
Rogers, eds., *The Political Economy* (Armonk, NY, 1984), 117–18.

[36]377 U.S. 533 (1964).

[37]Blacksher and Menefee, "At-Large Elections," at 221, "A constitutionally unacceptable flaw in the standards...is that they subordinate the
racial minority's right of judicial protection to the majority's right of electoral rule. Not only are blacks and other racial minorities required to carry
a heavier burden of proof than are majority groups in order to safeguard
for themselves an 'equally effective voice' in legislative apportionments, but
also the invidious intent standard [for racial discrimination only] actually
presumes that when majority voting strength is safeguarded the minority
has no further right to complain." See also note 25, above.

[38]*Fortson v. Dorsey,* 379 U.S. 433, 438–39 (1965); *Whitcomb v. Chavis,*
403 U.S. 124 (1971); *White v. Register,* 412 U.S. 755, 765 (1973); *City of
Mobile v. Bolden,* 446 U.S. 55 (1980) (upholding, unless proved intentionally discriminatory by direct evidence, at-large election of city officials in
city where blacks were one-third of electorate, and no black or black-
supported candidates were ever elected).

[39]By contrast, one-person-one-vote claims are successful based solely
on proof of mathematical inequality without regard to discriminatory purpose. *Karcher v. Daggett,* 102 S.Ct. 2653 (1984).

[40]42 U.S.C. §1973(b). The power to elect representatives is by its nature
a group power, since no individual voter can achieve her objective unless
joined by others supporting the same candidates. See Note, "Geometry and
Geography: Racial Gerrymandering and the Voting Rights Act," 94 Yale
L.J. 189, 198 (1984). Concern about diminution of the group-voting
strength of racial minorities is apparent from the statutory language and is
further elucidated in the legislative history. See, for example, S.Rep. No.
417, 97th Cong. 2d Sess. (1982).

[41]See note 38 above.

[42]*United States v. Carolene Products Co.,* 304 U.S. 144, 152, n.4 (1938).
"Prejudice against discrete and insular minorities may be a special condition...curtailing the operation of those political processes ordinarily to be
relied upon to protect minorities, and [so] may call for a correspondingly
more searching judicial inquiry."

[43]The 1965 Voting Rights Act, as amended in 1970, 1975, and 1982,
has been almost universally acclaimed as the most effective federal civil
rights statute ever passed, and it is credited with doubling in many southern
states the number of blacks registered to vote and multiplying tenfold the
number of black elected officials, at least in the first ten years after passage.
Recent gains have been more gradual, and some complain that, as the
numbers increased of blacks registered, voting, and getting elected, the
ingenuity also increased of incumbent white office holders who devised

sophisticated schemes to minimize merging black voting strength. For example, the number of U.S. attorney general objections to discriminatory election law changes actually doubled after 1975. 3 House Hearings, "Extension of the Voting Rights Act," 97th Cong., 1st sess., 2241–42.

44Most black elected officials are elected from majority black towns with populations of less than 1,000. Joint center for Political Studies, *1985 Roster of Black Elected Officials* (Washington, DC).

45Fiss, "Groups and the Equal Protection Clause," 5 Philosophy and Pub. Aff. 107, 152 (1976).

46Voting rights advocates always have seen the ballot as a tool for effective social change not only for blacks but also to advance a progressive agenda in general. See, for example, "Civil Rights No. 1–The Right to Vote," Martin Luther King, Jr., *New York Times* Sunday Magazine, March 14, 1965.

47*Gingles v. Edmisten,* 590 F. Supp. 345 (E.D. N.C. 1984) (three-judge court), prob. j. noted April 29, 1985, sub. nom. *Thornburg v. Gingles,* No. 83-1968.

48*Butts v. City of New York,* F. Supp. (S.D. N.Y. August 13, 1985), rev'd F.2d (2d Cir. 1985).

49*Perkins v. City of West Helena,* 675 F.2d 201, 212 (8th Cir. 1982).

50*Major v. Treen,* 574 F. Supp. 325 (E.D. La. 1983) (three-judge court); *Ketchum v. City Council of Chicago,* 740 F.2d 1398 (7th Cir. 1984), cert. denied U.S. (1985).

51J. Rogers, "The Politics of Voter Registration," *The Nation* (July 21–28, 1984): 45, 47.

52According to reports in the *New York Times,* "Fugitive Solidarity Official Calls Vote Boycott a Success," M. Kaufman, October 19, 1985, the underground Solidarity movement in Poland, claiming great success in its call for a boycott of parliamentary elections, challenged Polish government figures, saying that 40 percent of the electorate stayed home. The government published turn-out data showing 78 percent voting. By contrast, without any national political party officially proclaiming a boycott of elections, in recent years turnout in the United States has never even approached the putative Solidarity figures. The irony does not escape most commentators. As Professor Rogers explains, "In any country that claims to be a democracy, low electoral participation is an embarrassment. But the pattern of participation in the United States is more than that, because those who do vote are not representative of the population as a whole. The poorer and less educated segments of the population, clustered in low-paying jobs, vote at rates considerably less than their upscale cohorts." Rogers, "The Politics of Voter Registration," 47.

53"Voting for Democracy," a symposium jointly sponsored by the John F. Kennedy School of Government at Harvard University and the American Broadcasting Company, September 30–October 1, 1983, Washington, DC.

54See note 17, above.

55S. Lapidus, "Eradicating Racial Discrimination in Voter Registration: Rights and Remedies under the Voting Rights Act Amendment of 1982," 52 Fordham L. Rev. 93, 96 n.14 (1983).

56The constitutional bases of the cases rest on an equal protection claim, *Carrington v. Rash,* 386 U.S. 89 (1965); *Dunn v. Blumstein,* 405 U.S. 331 (1972), and the First Amendment's rejection of standardless licensing discretion, *Buckley v. Valeo,* 424 U.S. 1 (1976); *Iowa Socialist Party v. Slockett,* Civ. No. 83-190-D-1, F.Supp. (S.D. Iowa March 1, 1985). The Voting Rights Act claim is premised on the results test of Section 2 as amended in 1982.

57Other Western nations, such as Canada, facilitate registration, some of them using house-to-house canvassing similar to our census taking. "In Canada, which has a federal system similar to our own, 'enumerators' go to each household in each election district in urban areas. The canvassing takes place over a six-day period before each parliamentary election and the most recent reports indicate that 98 percent of all eligible voters in Canada were actually registered." Richard J. Carlson, "Personal Registration System Discourages Voter Participation," *National Municipal League* (December 1971), reproduced at Hearings of the House Committee on Post Office and Civil Service, 92d Cong. (92-51, 1972), Report at 414.

58It is especially important to keep our growing relationship with government in all spheres of existence apace with our evolving concepts of human dignity. The problems of the twentieth-century relationship of the citizen with government are explored by Associate Justice William J. Brennan, Jr., "The Constitution of the United States: Contemporary Ratification," Text and Teaching Symposium, Georgetown University, October 12, 1968, pp. 9–11.

59P. Chevigny, *New York Times,* July 23, 1984.

60"[E]lectorates are much more the product of political forces than many have appreciated, but also...to a considerable extent, they are political artifacts. Within limits, they can be constructed to a size and composition deemed desirable by those in power." Kelley, Ayres, and Bowen, "Registration and Voting: Putting First Things First," 67 APSR 359, 375 (1967).

61James Blacksher, Esquire, January 27, 1986, letter to C. Lani Guinier, on file with NAACP Legal Defense Fund.

Commentary to C. Lani Guinier

Justice Stanley Mosk

In this democratic society of ours do the people have an absolute right, without qualification of any kind, to vote for any person or any proposition? If such a right exists, or should exist, does it constructively serve democratic ends? The answers to those two questions must be hedged with numerous qualifications.

Any person has the right to go to the polls on election day and cast his vote, "but" first the person desiring to vote must meet certain qualifications: age (over eighteen), citizenship (American), prior registration, and in most jurisdictions no prior conviction of a felony. A second "but" applies to primary elections. Most states require registration in a political party in order to vote in that party's primary. Is this limitation permissible? A third "but" involves a right to vote by citizens who are not fluent in English. A federal act covers this situation for a limited number of states, although, in a majority, proficiency in English is required.

We want universal voting, but it is not an end in itself; it is merely a means to an end. The end is a democratically oriented government and ultimately a democratic society. To achieve that end, it is desirable that we achieve not mere voting, but rational voting.

Courts frequently have been called upon to help assure that the results of voting will reflect the true, reasoned, and informed choice of the people. All too often voting is based on incomplete information, without an understanding of the actual issues or in response to factors related to a candidate's fitness for office.

Not necessarily in order of importance, the following are some of the factors contributing to an irrational result. One factor that the public may not appreciate, but which most politicians understand all too well, is ballot placement—that is, the order in which the names appear on the electoral ballot. A number of courts, finding that a candidate listed first on the ballot (for offices other than president, governor, and senator) has a built-in advantage over his opponents, have struck down such procedures as violating the Fourteenth Amendment. *(McLain v. Meier* [8th Cir. 1980] 637 F.2d 1159) A random placement of the candidates is not much better. *(Clough v. Guzzi* [D. Mass. 1976] 416 F.Supp. 1057, 1068) The only fair method is for election officials to rotate the names of candidates in successive districts or precincts.

A second factor in irrational voting is caused by electioneering practices—that is, campaigning in or near polling places and last-minute smear attacks. These have brought about general regulations of the time, place, and manner of campaigning. Unfortunately, coercion, bribery, and intimidation of voters have a venerable history in this country. *(Fish v. Redecker* [Ariz. 1966] 411 Pac.2d 40)

Money also is a big factor in elections. Thus, statutes that require revelation of sources of campaign funds are helpful to the voter in assessing potential conflicts of interest. The voter who may be interested in deforestation projects should know, before voting, that a candidate who seeks his favor has received substantial contributions from lumber interests. *(Buckley v. Valeo* [1976] 424 U.S. 1) Along that same line are statutes requiring disclosure of the source of campaign material. A piece of literature that expresses views about candidates and issues should reveal its author so its value can be determined. *(Canon v. Justice Court* [1964] 61 Cal.2d 446, 458)

As for campaign funds, limitations on the amount that may be received from an individual or corporation have been upheld in some instances and rejected on First Amendment grounds in others. *First National Bank v. Bellotti* [1978] 435 U.S. 765) The problem involves a balancing between First Amendment rights, on the one hand, and hopeful achievement of election purity, on the other.

The U.S. Supreme Court's decision to strike down limits on campaign contributions and expenditures suggests that the Court may interpret the First Amendment as embodying the belief that voters can be counted on to act rationally, therefore the government has no compelling interest in restricting those forms of speech that might encourage irrational voting behavior. Thus, in *Bellotti,* the Court described the task of voters:

> [T]he people in our democracy are entrusted with the responsibility for judging and evaluating the relative merits of conflicting arguments. They may consider, in making their judgment, the source and credibility of the advocate. But if there be any danger that the

people cannot evaluate the information and arguments advanced by [a speaker], it is a danger contemplated by the Framers of the First Amendment.

In a more recent case, *Brown v. Hartlage* (456 U.S. 45, 60 [1982]), the Court stated that the First Amendment "embodies our trust in the free exchange of ideas as the means by which the people are to choose between...candidates for public office. The state's fear that voters might make an ill-advised choice does not provide the state with a compelling justification for limiting speech."

Another factor in intelligent voting is the ability of the voter to understand English, and the printing of ballots exclusively in English. In 1922, Justice Oliver Wendell Holmes remarked: "[I]t is desirable that all citizens of the United States should speak a common tongue." This statement may reflect a social policy that has existed in America from the inception of the nation, but the goal simply has not come to pass. An estimated 30 million persons, whose mother tongue is not English, reside in the United States. This figure represents over 11 percent of the population. Additional reports estimate that over 1 percent of the U.S. population speaks English not well or not at all. English illiteracy necessarily affects many aspects of life in the United States, including the right to vote.

In 1975, Congress addressed this problem of English illiteracy by amending the 1965 Voting Rights Act to establish a ten-year experiment, mandating the use of bilingual ballots and voting materials in certain geographical areas of the country. Congress subsequently extended the life of Federal Law Title 42, U.S. Code Section 1973aa-la, the bilingual ballot provision, to the year 1992. Many Californians did not agree with this federal action, and on November 6, 1984, they voiced their opinion through the passage of an initiative statute requiring the governor of California to write to the president of the United States, the U.S. attorney general, and all members of Congress a communication urging that ballots, voter pamphlets, and all other official voting materials be printed in English only.

Through express and implied provisions of the U.S. Constitution, the individual states traditionally have established voter qualifications for both state and federal elections (Article I, section 2 of the Constitution, and the Seventeenth Amendment). However, the right to control voter qualifications does not rest exclusively with the states. The right of a state to control federal elections is subject to congressional power under Article I, section 4 of the Constitution. In the 1932 case of *Smily v. Holm* (285 U.S. 355), Chief Justice Charles Evans Hughes interpreted the constitutional authority of

Congress over the election of U.S. senators and representatives to go far beyond the actual wording found in the Constitution. Hughes asserted that the comprehensive words of the provision imbued Congress with the authority to provide a complete code of congressional elections. Federal supremacy over state voter qualification authority was expanded by the 1969 Supreme Court ruling of *Kramer v. Union Free School District* (395 U.S. 621). In *Kramer,* the Court abandoned the traditional deferential review of the state voting statutes and announced that any device that burdens the right to vote should be subjected to strict scrutiny.

Amendments to the Constitution have placed additional restrictions on the ability of states to impose voting requirements. The Fifteenth Amendment prohibits states from impairing the franchise on the basis of race, color, or previous condition of servitude. The Nineteenth Amendment forbids sex discrimination in voting. The Twenty-fourth Amendment prevents the states from imposing any poll tax on a person before that person can vote for a candidate for a federal office, while the Twenty-sixth Amendment grants voting rights to all U.S. citizens who are eighteen years or older. Thus, the Constitution allocates to the states the right to make laws regarding state and national elections but provides that, if Congress becomes dissatisfied with the State laws, that body can alter them.

The use of a literacy test as a device to restrict certain minorities from the polls has had a long and pernicious history. A typical literacy test required all voter applicants to be able to read and write English before the applicants could exercise their right to vote. Many southern states included in their constitutions a "grandfather clause," which exempted white illiterates from the test because they were lineal descendants of persons entitled to vote on January 1, 1866. The use of a literacy test, coupled with a grandfather clause, allowed illiterate whites to vote but effectively denied the franchise to the majority of southern blacks until 1913, when the Supreme Court held that the use of a grandfather clause was unconstitutional.

This ruling, however, did not dissuade the use of state tests and, as late as 1960, the Supreme Court upheld the valid application of these tests. The case of *Lassiter v. Northampton County Board of Elections* (360 U.S. 45) upheld the literacy test in North Carolina by concluding that the ability to read and write has a rational relationship to standards designed to promote an intelligent use of the ballot. In reaching this conclusion, the Court reasoned that, although literacy and intelligence are not synonymous, the reliance of society on printed materials to canvass campaign issues may justify a state in allowing only those persons who are literate to exercise the franchise.

Five years later, however, the Court decided the cases of *United States v. Mississippi* (380 U.S. 128) and *Louisiana v. United States* (380 U.S. 145), in which it recognized the discriminatory use of these tests. The *Mississippi* and *Louisiana* decisions were given legislative support when Congress passed the 1965 Voting Rights Act prohibiting the discriminatory use of literacy tests wherever they had been used in the past. Finally, in 1970, Congress enacted a nationwide ban on all such tests. The constitutionality of this ban was upheld by the Supreme Court in *Oregon v. Mitchell* (400 U.S. 112).

Although the ban on literacy tests does not exclude the non-English-speaking citizen from the voting booth, an all-English ballot may work as effectively as the original literacy test in reducing voter participation in a discriminatory manner. Thus, Congress amended the 1965 Voting Rights Act by enacting 42 U.S.C. section 1973aa-1a.

This amendment mandates the use of bilingual voting ballots if two factors coexist. The first factor is met if the director of the census determines that more than 5 percent of the citizens of voting age in a state or political subdivision are members of a single-language minority. The second factor requires the English illiteracy rate of such persons as a group to be higher than the national rate. If both factors coexist, then the state or political subdivision must provide all voter information and materials, including ballots, in the applicable minority language as well as in English. This two-prong test was adopted by Congress to recognize that English-only voting materials, used in political subdivisions that contain no language minority citizens, do not act as a tool for discrimination and therefore should be allowed to continue.

The 1984 California initiative was a state declaration of public policy concerning the official use of the English language. The ultimate goal is the establishment of an "official" national language—not a novel suggestion. Although the Constitution contains no reference to choice of a national language, John Adams proposed the establishment of an English-language institute to promote its uniform use. This and similar proposals were rejected by the Framers as inconsistent with the social makeup of the young country. In 1917, Theodore Roosevelt actively campaigned for a uniform national language. He argued that, since there is but one flag, "we must also have but one language...we cannot tolerate any attempt to oppose or supplant the language and culture that has come down to us from the builders of this republic." In April 1981 a constitutional amendment that would establish English as the official language was proposed, but it found minimal support in Congress.

The implementation of an all-English ballot can be justified on several grounds. The first—and strongest—is the desire that all U.S. citizens speak a common language. An all-English voting ballot would promote this goal by motivating language minority citizens into full economic, social, and political life. In addition, the motivation to acquire the use of English would discourage the perpetuation of language ghettos currently found in many areas of the United States.

A second justification for the all-English ballot is that the present use of bilingual ballots is unnecessary. Advocates of this argument assert that, since all applicants for U.S. citizenship must pass a test for English proficiency, bilingual ballots are dispensable. The persuasiveness of the first and second arguments is increased when the financial burden of bilingual ballots, the third justification, is taken into account. For example, the 1982 cost of bilingual voting materials in California exceeded $1,200,000. These costs include the expense of translating, printing, and distributing ballots, sample ballots, and election pamphlets in various languages. Additional expenses for ballot counting also are foreseeable.

Finally, a fourth justification is that the current use of bilingual ballots in limited situations may be "inherently discriminatory." If equal protection of the law requires voting rights assistance to language minority citizens, then that assistance should be given to all language minorities and not just to those who reach a certain percentage of the overall population.

The current law mandating the establishment of a bilingual electoral system is supportable on a number of grounds. The first argument is that the use of bilingual ballots allows all citizens to live and participate in government free from discrimination. A second concerns notions of fundamental fairness. Bilingual assistance is needed for many citizens to cast their political vote effectively. American citizenship may be obtained with only a fifth-grade understanding of the English language. Many states, including California, consistently have complex initiative statements that must be understood and decided upon. Thus, a fifth-grade understanding of the English language clearly is insufficient to cast an effective ballot.

The third argument for the use of bilingual ballots is to increase the voter participation of language minority citizens. And finally, a fourth is that the cost and administrative complexities of a bilingual electoral system would not outweigh the constitutional right. Avoidance of administrative costs, although a valid concern, cannot justify imposition of otherwise improper legislation. Thus, strong arguments can be put forth both in support of and against the proposed English-only ballot.

Other aspects of rational voting include various devices used by politicians who have an insatiable desire to rule. One of the most common is the creation of friendly, or safe, districts. Sometimes this gerrymandering is done by drawing districts with political parties in mind—place Democrats here, Republicans there. Not infrequently this is done with race in mind—place all the blacks or Hispanics in one district and concede one legislator to them rather than have them scattered in several districts with the possibility of affecting several legislative seats. Another device is to elect all legislators at large, rather than from districts, and thus make an all-white result likely.

The validity of this latter procedure was the issue in a 1982 case before the U.S. Supreme Court. In *Rogers v. Lodge* (458 U.S. 613), black residents of Burke County, Georgia, claimed that the county commissioners' at-large election violated their Fourteenth and Fifteenth Amendment rights by diluting their voting power. While 38 percent of Burke County's voters were black, no black had ever been elected to the commission. While noting that all at-large elections tend to dilute minority voting strength because the majority readily can impose its will, the Court declared that such schemes are not unconstitutional per se, unless "conceived or operated as purposeful devices to further racial discrimination." *(Whitcomb v. Chavis* [1971] 403 U.S. 124)

This discriminatory intent need not be proved by direct evidence. However, the laundry list of evidentiary guidelines set down in *Zimmer v. McKiethen* (CA5 1973) 485 F.2d 1297, including past bias that precluded minorities' participation in elections, was held to be insufficient to show a discriminatory purpose by itself. Thus, it would not be enough for the district to have found that the absence of blacks on the commission was proof of bias. However, the district court amassed substantial other evidence of racial bias in the county's history and hence adequately buttressed its conclusion that the at-large system had been perpetuated to further racial discrimination.

Three justices dissented. Justice John Paul Stevens argued that the court failed to identify the constitutional standard for adjudicating such cases. He also said that the case-by-case "subjective intent" analysis approach used by the district court places too much power in the hands of the judiciary, usurping legislative prerogatives. He particularly criticized the district court's analysis of the county commission's motives, saying that the question of whose intentions control is ephemeral. "[I]f the standard the Court applies today extends to all types of minority groups, it is either so broad that virtually every political device is vulnerable or it is so undefined that federal judges can pick and choose almost at will among those that will be upheld and those that will be condemned."

Finally, Stevens argued that the court cannot apply a different standard to political groups organized on the basis of race from nonracial political interest groups. "A constitutional standard that [did so] would be inconsistent with the basic tenet of the Equal Protection clause. A permanent constitutional rule that treated them differently would, in my opinion, itself tend to perpetuate race as a feature distinct from all others; a trait that makes persons different in the eyes of the law."

Absentee voting often creates additional problems. A 1983 New Jersey case is illustrative. In *Battle* (46b A.2d 1291), the plaintiff lost an election by twenty-four votes. She claimed the election was void because, in the case of seventy-four absentee ballots returned in person, the messenger had failed to sign the outside envelope or had failed to sign a county log of all hand-returned absentee ballots, in violation of a statutory requirement. Without invalidating the election, the court held that the absentee ballots were cast improperly and remanded the case to a lower court to determine the election's validity.

The court held that, while state election law was "intended to protect the voter," a review of the legislative history showed that lawmakers intended to strike a balance between enhancing voting rights and ensuring the integrity of elections. "Moreover, although we agree that disenfranchisement of a voter is an end reasonably to be avoided, it must be kept in mind that the statutory right to vote as an absentee is not an absolute right and is subject to proper legislative exception and limitation." The court held that absentee voting is a privilege and not a right, although state law requires liberal construction of statutes to allow absentees to vote. Because the public election scheme is a creature of statute, not common law, the statute's express language must govern.

This may portend some future elections: voting by mail. That was the issue in *Peterson v. City of San Diego,* a case heard by our court in 1983. (34 Cal.3d 225) San Diego authorized a special election by mail so that voters could approve or disapprove a convention center lease arrangement. The city mailed voters ballots fourteen days before the election; voters then could mail the ballots back or place them in three locked boxes around the city by midnight of election day. The plaintiff contended that the state constitution requires casting votes in secret. Otherwise, the door would be opened to vote buying or other coercion as voters could show other interested parties how they voted.

The court held that the procedure met the constitutional requirement. First, the court declared that the procedure was analogous to absentee voting, which had been done by mail for more than sixty years. Second, it said that mail voting serves two important policy purposes: voter participation increases due to increased convenience, and special elections cost much less. Further, criminal penalties attached to vote manipulation would deter would-be manipulators. The court emphasized that voting was fundamental to representative government and should be facilitated whenever possible.

Two concurring judges thought that mail voting increased the likelihood of "subtle forms of coercion," such as interest-group vote-marking parties and spouses voting in each other's presence. They said, however, that in this case the interest in greater participation outweighed these reservations, but they withheld judgment on mail voting's overall constitutionality.

A somewhat more frequently recurring issue is the right of a citizen to vote in a party primary when he is not registered in that party. On the one hand, it is argued that, since the state governs the election process in party primaries, any citizen in the state should have the right to vote in any party election as he sees fit. On the other hand, it is contended that political parties have an associational right to choose their candidates and issues and in that process to limit participation to those who share the ideology of the party. The latter point of view prevails in most states.

Another issue is the right of freedom of association, derived from the First Amendment and guaranteeing free speech, the right to peaceably assemble, and the right to petition for redress of grievances. Freedom of association confers a right to join with others to pursue activities independently protected by the First Amendment. In *NAACP v. Alabama* (357 U.S. 449), for example, the Court "recognized the vital relationship between freedom to associate and privacy in one's associations." The Court also looked to effects on the association's ability to advocate the beliefs of its members. In protecting the ability of NAACP "members to pursue their *collective* effort to foster beliefs," the Court implicitly recognized that an association may be able to achieve objectives so far beyond individual capability as to be different qualitatively, and it ruled that the Constitution protects the ability of such an association to carry out the First Amendment activities of its members. Freedom of association confers on each member the right to combine and take advantage of an association whose whole may be greater than the sum of its parts.

Because the First Amendment protects political advocacy and participation in partisan politics, freedom of association necessarily includes a right of political association that protects the right to form a political party for the advancement of partisan political beliefs. One way political parties advance shared beliefs is by selecting candidates representing those beliefs to run in a general election.

The right to vote encompasses yet another issue: that of individuals seeking public office. It involves the ability to place one's name on the ballot as a candidate. This significant right was vindicated in the case of *Anderson v. Celebrezze,* decided by the U.S. Supreme Court in 1983. (103 S.Ct. 1564) On April 24, 1980, Representative John Anderson announced that he was an independent candidate for the presidency of the United States. Thereafter, he met all of the substantive requirements for having his name placed on the ballot in all fifty states and the District of Columbia for the November 1980 general election. By that time, however, it was too late for Anderson to qualify for a position on the Ohio ballot because the statutory deadlines for filing a statement of candidacy had passed. Anderson and three Ohio voters challenged the constitutionality of Ohio's early filing deadline.

The Court agreed with Anderson's arguments on all counts. Specifically, the Court found that the Ohio filing deadline: 1) burdened the First Amendment associational rights of independent voters and candidates; 2) placed significant state-imposed restrictions on the nationwide electoral process; 3) discriminated against candidates and voters whose political preferences lie outside existing political parties; and 4) implicated a uniquely important national interest in that the president and vice-president are the only elected officials who represent all voters in the United States and, hence, the impact of the votes cast in each state affects the votes cast in other states.

The Court set forth a strict scrutiny test to be applied by courts in resolving constitutional challenges to state election laws. First, the court must balance the character and magnitude of the asserted injury against the rights protected by the First and Fourteenth Amendments that the plaintiff seeks to vindicate. Second, the court must identify and evaluate the precise interests asserted by the state, including the legitimacy, strength, and necessity of those interests, to justify the burden imposed by its rule. Applying this balancing test, the Court found that the Ohio filing deadline burdened the First Amendment associational rights of independent voters and candidates.

Applying the second part of the balancing test, the Court in *Anderson* identified and handily rejected each of Ohio's asserted interests. Ohio first claimed that the deadline allowed a longer time for voter education. The Court held that it would be unrealistic in this age of modern telecommunications to think that it would take more than seven months to inform the electorate about a candidate just because he lacked a party label.

Ohio next claimed that it was providing equal treatment for partisan and independent candidates alike, since a candidate participating in a primary election had to declare his or her candidacy on the same date as an independent. The Court found that both the burdens and benefits of the respective requirements were materially different and that the reasons for early filing for a primary candidate were inapplicable to independent candidates. And third, Ohio contended that the filing deadline preserved the stability of the state political system.

A somewhat similar problem occurred some years earlier in *Storer v. Brown,* another case that reached the U.S. Supreme Court. (415 U.S. 724) Four federal office candidates sued after various provisions of the California Elections Code denied them space on the ballot. Two were disqualified under section 6830, subd. (d), which denies an independent candidate ballot space if he registered with a qualified political party within one year prior to the immediately preceding primary election. Two others, inveterate Communist party candidate Gus Hall and his running mate on the presidential ticket, were disqualified because they could not meet the requirements of sections 6831 and 6833. (Section 6831 requires an independent candidate's nominating papers to be signed by between 5 and 6 percent of the entire vote cast in the preceding general election, while section 6833 requires these signatures—some 325,000 in Hall's case—to be gathered in a set twenty-four-day period. Furthermore, none of the signers can be people who voted in the primary.)

The Court upheld the constitutionality of section 6830, subd. (d), against First and Fourteenth Amendment challenges but ordered further proceedings in the district court to find whether sections 6831 and 6833 unconstitutionally restricted them from the ballot. While acknowledging that the law requires states to provide ways for non-Republicans or non-Democrats to appear on the ballot, the Court deferred to laws that serve a particularized legitimate purpose and are not arbitrary. The Court then appeared to be more preoccupied with the state's interest in orderly elections than with the rights of voters or candidates to maximize choice: "California apparently believes with the Founding Fathers that splintered parties and unrestrained factionalism may do significant damage to the fabric of government. It appears to us that the one-year disaffiliation provision furthers the State's interest in the stability of its political system." The Court did not wish to "sacrifice the political stability of the system of the State, with profound consequences for the entire citizenry, merely in the interest of particular candidates and their supporters having instantaneous access to the ballot." (415 U.S. at 736)

Three justices rejected this profoundly conservative view of the relation between citizens and state, noting that the law required the plaintiffs to "take affirmative action toward candidacy fully 17 months before the general election. That is an impossible burden to shoulder." Even accepting the majority's view that preventing electoral factionalism is a "compelling" state interest, the dissenters noted that "compelling state interests may not be pursued by 'means that unnecessarily burden or restrict constitutionally protected activity' when less onerous alternatives exist." (415 U.S. at 760)

In the case of Hall and his running mate, who were required to amass 325,000 signatures of nonprimary voters within twenty-four days following the primary, the court analyzed the law to surmise that substantially more than 5 percent of the voter pool would have to sign for Hall to qualify, and that this might well be an unconstitutional burden. The California requirement, if correctly analyzed, "would be in excess, percentagewise, of anything the Court has approved to date as a precondition to an independent's securing a place on the ballot." The majority remanded the case for the district court to do the actual analysis.

The majority rejected the state's argument that Hall and his running mate could have gotten on the ballot by qualifying a new political party, a procedure that only requires 1 percent of the voters in the last gubernatorial election to have filed affiliation statements with the county clerks, or if the new party files a petition with signatures constituting 10 percent of the last gubernatorial vote. (Elections Code §6430) The court held that forming a new political party is entirely different from running on the ballot as an independent, both from the voter and candidate's standpoint. Voters affiliating with the new party would surrender their ties to another or as an independent, while candidates would have to meet numerous formalities surrounding the formation of political parties. An independent candidate should not be forced to form or join a party, the court held.

Another rather complicated voting problem arises in connection with municipal annexations. For example, Area A wants to be annexed to City B, or conversely, City B seeks to annex Area A. Who votes on these proposals—both the area and the city, or only the city's residents? How about absentee landowners whose property and taxes may be directly affected by annexation?

A proposed annexation, if consummated, is likely to affect significantly residents of both the annexing and the annexed areas. In part, this impact is economic. One common reason for annexation is fiscal: a municipality seeks to annex a region beyond its boundaries so that the new area's tax base can be tapped for the city's needs. Municipalities also may seek to annex potential sites of urban growth in order to regulate the course which that growth will take; the outcome of the annexation election thus will affect regulation of land use in the annexed areas and the impact of growth upon both areas. Since municipal utilities have a duty to provide services on an equal basis to those within those boundaries, a successful annexation will result in an expansion of municipal services to the annexed area, with an increase in the burden to municipal agencies. Beyond these economic effects, annexation has a significant impact upon the political interests of the residents of both areas.

Despite annexation's impact on the economic and political interests of residents of both areas, some statutes permit annexation to be accomplished in an election limited to residents of only one area. Whether the franchise is limited to residents of the annexing municipality (as in Missouri) or residents of the annexed area (as in Ohio), it is apparent that a group of citizens whose interests will be significantly affected by the outcome of the annexation election is being excluded from voting in that election.

Voting rights cases decided by the Supreme Court suggest that such unequal access to the franchise may violate the equal protection clause unless justified by a significant state interest. *(Dunn v. Blumstein,* 405 U.S. 303) The basis for this constitutional protection of the vote seems to be twofold. The opportunity to participate in elections is a crucial expression of "the democratic ideals of equality and majority rule." *(Reynolds v. Sims,* 377 U.S. 533, 566) Along with its symbolic significance, the vote has obvious practical importance as a means of influencing policy and protecting the voter's interests. The Court's guarantee of an equal vote, first applied in *Reynolds* to reject malapportionment of state legislatures, has been extended to governments at the local level.

Ever since the innovative days of Governor Hiram Johnson, California has had the initiative, a means by which the voters directly may adopt legislation. The scheme was designed originally as a method of giving people control of their own destiny. Their fate previously had been held hostage by railroad barons, land speculators, and financial institutions that controlled the state and its public officials. Corruption was deemed to be indigenous to the body politic. For most of this century the initiative appears to have served the people well, but it has now fallen into the hands of a new type of speculator: the initiative promoter. Using computerized techniques of fund-raising and petition circulating, these promoters seek an emotional issue at every election, and as a result they have an inordinate effect upon state and local government.

To illustrate part of the problem, when a statute is proposed in the legislature it is considered by a committee in one house, debated on the floor of that house, considered by a committee in the other house, debated on the floor of the other house, and finally sent to the governor, who has his veto opportunity. In that lengthy sifting process, the flaws, conflicts, and internal ambiguities generally are discovered and ironed out. In contrast, any two of us can sit down at a typewriter, peck out an initiative that may have drastic effects on the lives of millions of Californians, give it a seductive title—say, "for better government and lower taxes"—and engage a professional promoter to obtain the signatures to place the proposal on the ballot. The problem is that we may have hit some wrong keys on the typewriter.

Our own court has had to interpret a measure that used "and" instead of "or" in one clause, which completely frustrated the very purpose advocated by the sponsors. In other instances we have found serious half-truths in an interpretation of constitutional requirements. Yet, when such flaws are brought to the attention of the courts and courts are obliged on constitutional grounds to invalidate part or all of an initiative, the judges often are flogged for thwarting the will of the people.

A second aspect of initiative proposals causes anguish to voters and to the judiciary: instances in which the voters are not entitled to vote on the measure because of its patent invalidity. Some persons contend that courts should never bar a measure from the ballot but let the people vote and consider potential unconstitutionality later. As a general proposition, that may be sound. However, to give an extreme example, suppose the Church of Scientology circulates a petition and obtains enough signatures thereon to declare Scientology the official religion of California. Should courts allow that matter to be voted on, with all the divisiveness such a campaign would cause, when the measure facially violates the Constitution? I would hope not.

Our court received widespread criticism and accusations of partisanship when we barred from the ballot an initiative that would have reapportioned legislative districts. The problem was that the Constitution provides for only one reapportionment after each decennial census, and the one for this decade already had been adopted.

A number of suggestions to reform our initiative process are emanating from respected nonpartisan groups like the League of Women Voters. The initiative should never be abandoned, for it is truly an important safety valve for the people, although I might ask rhetorically: when was the last time you can recall an initiative truly originating at the grass roots rather than from some special interest? As a result, some reforms should be considered. For example, perhaps an initiative measure should be sent to the California legislature for debate, and possible amendment, on details as distinguished from substance, before submission to the people. Perhaps there should be more regulations of professional promoters and political fund-raisers. At least, we should give some thought to reforms in this vital area of political life.

Reflections on the U.S. Constitution: A Conversation with William F. Buckley, Jr.*

Is the Constitution relevant in the late twentieth century?

BUCKLEY: It is for some people. Others believe that it is simply available as a well-tempered scale on which to improvise, and for so long as the mathematical intervals between the notes are kept intact they can go ahead and read whatever music they want. Others go further and say that the Constitution incorporates an ideal, the explication of which responsible judicial scholarship should undertake to continue as a perpetual challenge. I like to think of it as relevant in the latter rather than the former sense.

Is our constitutional republic a model for other nations, and should it be?

BUCKLEY: The question of whether any particular country's constitution is a paradigm has been posed for hundreds of years. Rousseau at some point was asked to write a model constitution, as others have been. I think that scholarship increasingly vindicates the notion that, although our Constitution utters and pursues certain universals, the mechanical accommodations incorporated in it are cultural reflections rather than notions that should automatically apply in every other situation. If one asks, would I—had I the power to—export the Constitution exactly as it exists to every other country in the world, the answer is, I would not. However, I absolutely would insist that the relationships of human beings to each other and to their government that are incorporated in the Constitution are universal.

*Interview with John A. Moore, Jr., California State Polytechnic University, Pomona, April 9, 1986.

Is the Constitution too restraining, or not restraining enough?

BUCKLEY: This question would amuse people who have used it as the most pliable instrument since Silly Putty. I cannot think of anything in the Constitution that restrained Justice Blackmun when he suddenly decided it would be all right to protect abortion, or anything in the Constitution that persuaded the Supreme Court that the commerce clause should be permitted to govern rules affecting elevators in the state of Ohio. So, the answer is, it is not; it has not been restraining during the past thirty or forty years. Indeed, I think it should be more restraining; in the absence of which there is the alternative of modifying it explicitly.

Can legitimate policies be implemented in a timely fashion under the Constitution?

BUCKLEY: The question of whether legitimate policies can be undertaken under the Constitution puts all of the gravity of the sentence on the word "legitimate." Some people might consider illegitimate what Franklin Delano Roosevelt did in 1939, 1940, and 1941, which, in my judgment, was unconstitutional. He maneuvered toward a warlike situation by making certain clandestine deals with Churchill and others. The question one ultimately has to ask is whether there was a historical vindication for treating the Constitution with certain artistic license, which almost exclusively falls under the aegis of the executive—that is, the legislature cannot very well improvise in chambers, while the executive can. And we wait for the historians and the scholars to ask whether there was an abuse of power of the kind that invalidates the legitimate restraints of the Constitution.

Have we used the Constitution to overemphasize individual rights at the expense of common purposes?

BUCKLEY: Whether we have overemphasized individual rights under the Constitution is a question concerning which one can give different answers in different situations. If the Constitution is interpreted as saying, as Justice Black would have said, that one cannot pass any law whatsoever restraining expressions of opinion of any kind—therefore, one cannot have antipornography laws or antilibel laws—then my opinion is, yes. Paradoxically, I do not think that this is a defense of the individual. It is an affront to individual rights. In the case of libel, for instance, your right to say whatever you want about me may appear to be an exercise in subsidizing your rights. In effect, it is an act of derogating mine. It depends on the area that we are addressing.

Does the Constitution aid special interests over the common good?

BUCKLEY: This question is, I think, moot. The Constitution is explicitly indifferent to that particular question, except to the extent that it insists on parity among individual states in the Senate. I do think the special interests have tended in the last fifteen or twenty years to dominate legislation, but this is a development that one cannot blame on the Constitution.

One must recognize that not all that long ago the vote was by no means the expression of liberty in which the Constitution was primarily interested. We are about to celebrate the 100th anniversary of the Statue of Liberty, and no one thought it a great hypocrisy to depict as a land of liberty a country in which blacks had only de jure but not de facto manumission and women no vote at all. As the vote became the principal instrument of liberty, it became an instrument used substantially for effecting the distribution of budgetary largesse and, as such, emphases were changed which were not foreseen by the Constitution. It is for that reason that some people say that we now need another constitutional amendment imposing a limit on deficit spending.

Has the expansion of democratic participation under the Constitution resulted in better government?

BUCKLEY: I do not know any way in which one could inquire into that question. In the first place, one would have to define what better government was. There is a solid difference of opinion, often ideologically based, on whether one has better government or not. It is true that Democrats were the primary enthusiasts for extending the vote to eighteen-year-olds and were overwhelmed with dismay when they discovered, having done so, that the majority of eighteen-year-olds voted for the Republican party. But we see the participation net sinking year after year. I think something like 18 or 20 percent fewer people voted in the last election than voted in the Eisenhower election in 1952. I find no grounds whatever for any correlation between the extent of participation and the democratic exercise, on the one hand, and the commendability of the product, on the other.

What has been the impact of the mass media on this constitutional republic? Has the impact been good or bad?

BUCKLEY: The media are antideliberative. The kind of reactions stimulated by the mass media, which it is their business to stimulate since they are naturally attracted to melodrama, accents issues which are antideliberative in nature. For that reason, I regret that influence, having no idea whatsoever of any means by which the effect can be mitigated.

You are probably the Conservative movement's chief spokesman. Are you satisfied at the success of conservativism and do you see this as being long-lasting, or will there be another wave of liberalism?

BUCKLEY: I would answer with a qualified "yes." I think that the nostrums of liberalism will be looked at skeptically for a generation to come. That is a very solid achievement. On the other hand, I do not believe that the Conservative movement has effected anything like totally reliable consensus on certain points that I think are extremely important. And I do not mind confessing that one of them is the philosophical virility of the idea of a progressive income tax. It is singled out by Friedrich Hayek as the Achilles' heel of American democracy. He may very well be right. Although substantial progress has been made in not supposing that higher and higher taxation is socially progressive, I am by no means convinced of the opposite, namely, that there is a consensus on the point that progressive income taxation itself lies on philosophically shaky ground.

What changes in the Constitution would you recommend?

BUCKLEY: I think the time definitely has come for countering the tendency to block voting by imposing a limit on the deficit. It should be properly hedged by permitting an overruling by a very solid majority in the House of Representatives. That is an amendment to the Constitution that I would welcome. As a matter of fact, I should confess that I would like to see any constitutional amendment at this point that overturns the Supreme Court on almost any issue, simply because we need to penetrate the superstition that the Supreme Court is reliable and, indeed, a supreme moral tribunal.

What one thing about the Constitution do you believe is the most valuable?

BUCKLEY: This is easy to answer. One needs and should have access to a body of codified thought to which one can appeal against legislative or executive caprice.

The Attorney General, the Declaration, the Constitution, and Original Intent

Harry V. Jaffa

In a speech at Dickinson College on September 17, 1985—Constitution Day—Attorney General Edwin Meese discussed the principles of the Constitution, in precisely the sense in which I have reproached him for not having done so. This I am pleased to acknowledge, while lamenting the fact that this discussion seems not to have developed the coherence and sustained power and influence that its importance warrants. The attorney general, while setting forth a position consistent with the tradition of Thomas Jefferson, James Madison, and Abraham Lincoln, appears not to be aware that it is a contested position, and one denied, if that were possible, more vigorously and emphatically by present-day Conservatives than by their Liberal counterparts. Meese does not seem to realize that further efforts of the kind represented by his speech are necessary, and that the charitable work of conversion to its doctrine must begin at home, in the Department of Justice and among the jurists to whom he turns for judicial nominees. It is the publicists and jurists of contemporary conservatism who owe far more allegiance to John C. Calhoun than to Jefferson and Lincoln.

Meese calls the principles of the Declaration of Independence "our most ennobling principles" and rightly insists that they are the genuine principles of the Constitution. Of the rights asserted in the Declaration, he says that they "existed *in nature* before governments and laws were ever formed." (Emphasis by Meese) "As the physical world is governed by natural laws such as gravity," he continues, "so the political world is governed by other natural laws in the form of natural rights." Meese at this point, however, would elicit the patronizing smiles of the sophisticates for confusing the two senses of "government," for it does indeed have a radically different meaning, as applied to the physical world, from that applied to the moral or political world. The laws of gravity are invariant relations subsisting between matter and motion. To state that these relations are "laws" is merely to say that they are invariable. We say that objects are attracted by a force proportional to the product of their masses and inversely proportional to the square of the distance between them. To state that they do so because they ought to do so is indeed essentially meaningless. There is no "ought" in respect to such behavior, only an "is."

The propositions of the Declaration of Independence, however, are so far from describing actual behavior that it may be doubted whether, on July 4, 1776, there existed anywhere in the world—except in the United States—a government that genuinely derived its "just powers" from the "consent of the governed." (After that date Americans were far less willing than they had been before it to credit the British constitution with being such a government.) The Declaration, from beginning to end, is a document of the "ought" rather than the "is," one that is prescriptive rather than descriptive of human and political behavior. The behavior it describes (namely, the tyrannical behavior of the British government) is described, for the most part, to be condemned. Meese recognizes this distinction somewhat vaguely when he says, paraphrasing Jefferson, that "these natural rights [those belonging to men by the laws of nature] were left unsecured by nature," and therefore "governments are instituted among men." According to Meese, "There exists in the nature of things a natural standard for judging whether governments are legitimate or not." But since ancient times men have wondered at the fact, as Aristotle observed in Athens, "that fire burns the same here and in Persia," while things called just are everywhere different. From this many, including nearly all present-day Conservatives and Liberals, have concluded that nature is not and cannot be a standard "for judging whether governments are legitimate or not." While the attorney general and I are in agreement here, he writes as if others also agreed with us. By and large, they do not. He should realize that he must argue his case for the Declaration's "laws of nature and of nature's God" on grounds altogether different from those of the laws of gravity.

Scarcely a law or philosophy professor in the United States today accepts the idea that there is a standard in nature for judging either men or governments. Nature as a ground of right is thought to be a myth exploded by the progress of modern science—that same science that discovered the laws of gravity. The essence of those laws is that they express something "that is everywhere the same" and do not raise any questions of the "ought" variety. In the progress of this same science, it is believed, it has been discovered that all species, man included, have evolved from lower forms of life by an essentially accidental and purposeless process. Biological nature, man included, is nothing but the result of a struggle for survival, with nothing normative but the goal of survival itself. Evolution recognizes no other standard but survival, and to survive means to be victorious. As far as nature is concerned, justice then is nothing but the interest of the stronger.

Thus Carl Becker, in his famous 1922 book on the Declaration, expressed the opinion that is still predominant when he said: "To ask whether the natural rights philosophy of the Declaration of Independence is true or false is essentially a meaningless question." Concerning Jefferson's assertion that the doctrines of the Declaration represented "the common sense of the subject," Becker wrote that "what seems but common sense in one age often seems but nonsense in another." There is, in short, no permanent framework of meaning, such as nature, within which moral or political truths can be grasped. The only genuine framework is a changing one, best denominated "history." The only permanent knowledge of right and wrong is the knowledge that all such knowledge is impermanent. That there are eternal truths—the ground of the convictions of the Signers and of the principles of the Constitution—is an illusion. That this is so, said Becker, "is the fate which has overtaken the sublime truths enshrined in the Declaration of Independence."

Becker and those of his mind—and they continue to dominate our universities and especially our law schools—have remained steadfast in the conviction that what appeared to be truth, or nature, in one age represents nothing more than "the climate of opinion" of that age. All so-called truths (as in "We hold these truths") then are true only relative to the "spirit" or the "climate of opinion" of an age. But neither Becker nor any of the other representatives of this relativism have doubted that such relativism is itself a final truth and not merely expressive of the spirit of our present age. They hold with the finality of death itself to the proposition "We hold this truth to be self-evident, that all truth is relative." They are all epigones of the mythical—but no less real for being mythical—Cretan, the first modern philosopher, who declared that all Cretans are liars. Therefore, if Becker could continue to refer to the "sublime truths" of the Declaration, he did so meaning no more than that they continued to seem sublime and true *to him*. He did not for a moment consider them to be sublime and true *in themselves*. It is only in the latter sense, however, that anyone can believe that the principles of the Declaration can be "laws of nature."

In the course of his speech, Meese continues, explaining that

this theory of government, this philosophy of natural rights, is what made the institution of slavery intolerable.... It is a common view that the Framers of the Constitution made concessions to slavery. ...But that rather common view is, in fact, a common mistake. The Constitution did not make fundamental concessions to slavery at the level of principle. Nowhere in the Constitution do the words "slavery" or "slave" appear. Indeed the framers of the Constitution, while forced by political realities to *tolerate* slavery for a while *in practice,* never *accepted* that "peculiar institution" *in principle.* (Emphasis by Meese)

What he states here is essentially the position taken by Lincoln, but, as Meese stresses, it is not the common view, nor is it evidently the right view. It is a position that requires an argument that, like Lincoln's, is both systematic and tenacious.

Meese makes much of the fact that the words "slave" and "slavery" do not occur in the Constitution. Madison, we know, did say that the words had been kept out of the document so that when the institution disappeared it would leave no mark behind it. That was a pious hope, however, rather than a benchmark of the Framers' handiwork. "Three fifths of all other Persons" in Article I, section 2, refers unmistakably to black slaves and can never be understood differently, nor can this increase in the representation of slaveowners, relative to that of free persons in free states, be understood merely as toleration. It clearly strengthens the political power of slavery among the factions comprehended by that "extended republic" of the "more perfect Union." (The fact that "direct taxes" as well as "representatives" are "apportioned" together does not constitute a balancing justification, since the representation is an operating consequence of the Constitution, while the taxes are merely a contingent possibility, one that never came into effect before the Civil War. Furthermore, it is the House, in which the slaveowners are overrepresented, in which the taxes must originate.)

The most powerful evidence of slavery within the Constitution, however, is in Article IV, section 2:

No person held to service. or labor in one State, under the laws thereof, escaping into another, shall, in consequence of any law or regulation therein, be discharged from such service or labor, but shall be delivered up on claim of the party to whom such service or labor may be due.

This is preceded by the "full faith and credit," the "privileges and immunities," and the criminal extradition clauses. All three are modeled, with only minor variations, upon parallel passages in Article IV of the Articles of Confederation. But there is no parallel in the Articles for the fugitive slave clause of the Constitution. From such evidence it would certainly appear that the "more perfect Union" was more greatly committed to the perpetuation of slavery than was its predecessor.

The Constitution, by reason of the fugitive slave clause, became a vehicle for the enforcement of state laws for the protection of slave property. By assigning to the United States a constitutional duty to enforce these laws, the Constitution made the United States a party to them. State law became to this extent a part of the constitutional law. The laws of the slave states regarded slaves at one and the same time as chattel property and as human persons, notwithstanding that by logical necessity persons cannot be chattels and chattels cannot be persons. The Constitution calls the slaves "persons held to service or labor," although everyone knew that they were so held, not as persons but as chattels. The Constitution thereby becomes a party to a conspiracy to dehumanize these persons into chattels, even as it calls them persons.

Even worse, however, section 4 of Article IV states that

the United States shall guarantee to every State in this Union a republican form of government, and shall protect each of them against invasion; and on application of the legislature, or of the executive (when the legislature cannot be convened) against domestic violence.

Has not the attorney general subscribed, without equivocation, to the doctrine that a republican form of government is one based upon the proposition that all men are created equal, that all human beings are equally endowed with unalienable rights, and that the just powers of government are derived from the consent of the governed? Certainly a republican form of government is even more than this, but it can be no less. Yet none of these conditions was met by the slave states, in which the slaves were governed without their consent, and by laws altogether different from those by which the masters, or free whites generally, governed themselves. Still, the Constitution presumes them to be republican. How could it have done so?

Do we then abandon the Declaration's definition of republicanism? If not, what meaning do we assign to this "guarantee" of a republican form of government? The guarantee, moreover, takes on a peculiarly sinister meaning when we see it linked to the requirement that the United States protect each state "against domestic violence." That meant, as everyone in 1787 knew, against any attempt by the slaves to throw off the yoke of their masters, as their masters had thrown off the yoke of the British. The right of revolution is the sanction for all rights proclaimed in the Declaration of Independence. It is the guarantee of all guarantees of a "republican form of government." "Any people anywhere," said Lincoln in 1848, "being inclined and having the power, have the *right* to rise up and shake off the existing government.... This is a most valuable, a most sacred right—a right which, we hope and believe, is to liberate the world." Yet the effective denial of this very right, in the Constitution, is linked with the guarantee of a republican form of government.

Surely contradiction is here carried to its uttermost limits. Article IV of the Constitution not only obliges the government of the United States to return the runaway slave to his master but also obliges it to assist the master in suppressing any attempts the slave may make for freedom where the United States has compelled him to remain. Here at least we can understand why Calhoun has appeared so plausible in his denial that the principles of the Declaration had any weight in constructing the American governments following the Revolution. The attorney general, then, must recognize that far more is required of him than the simple assertion that the Constitution makes no fundamental concessions to slavery at the level of principle. That assertion is difficult to maintain in the face of the evident and original meaning of Article IV. It can be maintained only by unswerving commitment to the truth of the principles of the Declaration of Independence, and by unrelenting resistance to legal positivism and to the philosophical nihilism that lies behind it.

Meese, in defending the antislavery character of the original Constitution, says that it "made explicit provision for a time in the not-so-distant future when Congress could seek to restrict not only the slave trade but the institution itself." This is a very loose and inexact reference to Article I, section 9, which reads, in part: "The migration or importation of such persons as any of the States now existing shall think proper to admit, shall not be prohibited by the Congress prior to the year one thousand eight hundred and eight."

This unrepealable provision not only does not prohibit the foreign slave trade but also forbids the prohibition of that trade by Congress for twenty years. It permits—but does not require—Congress to prohibit that trade thereafter. To remind ourselves what this trade was, we should recur to Jefferson's original draft of the

Declaration, and his characterization of the king of England for permitting its continuance:

> He has waged cruel war against human nature itself, violating its most sacred rights of life and liberty in the persons of a distant people who never offended him, captivating and carrying them into slavery in another hemisphere, or to incur miserable death in their transportation thither. This piratical warfare, the opprobrium of infidel powers, is the warfare of the Christian King of Great Britain.

Yet this same "piratical warfare" was to go on for at least another twenty years, under the absolute protection of the Constitution. The influx of slaves under that protection during those years has been estimated to be nearly as great as the importation during the previous 160 years. With the benefit of hindsight, it can be said that the Civil War would never have happened had not the Framers blundered as they did on this provision. There is no basis whatever for the attorney general's remark that by this clause the Constitution seeks to restrict "not only the slave trade but the spread of the institution itself." When, in 1809, Congress outlawed the foreign slave trade, it did so in part because of the votes of the older border slave states—Maryland, Delaware, Virginia, and Kentucky. These states were anxious to see the end of that trade, not for humanitarian reasons but because they wished protection for their profitable trade in selling their surplus slaves to the expanding economies of the states of the Deep South: Georgia, Alabama, Mississippi, and Louisiana. Cheap foreign imports lowered the prices at which they could sell and thereby lowered the profits from their sales. Meese could hardly have made a more unfortunate choice to exhibit the anti-slavery principles of the Constitution.

"The issue in *Dred Scott,*" the attorney general writes, "was not whether slavery was right or wrong but only whether Congress had the legitimate power to keep it out of the new territories. Congress and Lincoln and Dred Scott said Congress did have that power. The Supreme Court said it did not. By declaring the Missouri Compromise unconstitutional, the Court, in the view of some, made war inevitable." At this time, however, Congress did not say that it had the power to keep slavery out of the territories. In the Kansas-Nebraska Act of 1854, Congress had repealed the Missouri Compromise restriction of slavery. This it had done three years before the Taney Court declared such a restriction unconstitutional. During the Mexican War the House repeatedly passed the Wilmot Proviso, which declared slavery to be unlawful in any territory that the United States might acquire from Mexico in consequence of the war. But the Senate never agreed, and the Proviso never became law. In the Compromise of 1850 slavery was not outlawed in the new territories; it was provided that new states, to be formed out of the new territories, would decide at the time they applied for admission into the Union whether they would be free or slave. Nothing was said concerning the crucial question of the status of slavery in the territories during the period before they were qualified to become states.

Questions concerning property rights involving slaves, however, might be appealed from the territorial courts directly to the Supreme Court of the United States. Here was the germ of the case of *Dred Scott.* Congress could not make up its mind, or rather there was no consensus on the question in Congress upon which it could act. Therefore, this supremely political question was placed at the door of what should have been the most unpolitical branch of the government. It is true that *Dred Scott* involved the territorial legislation of 1820 instead of 1850. But, as Congress already had repealed the 1820 legislation, the Court could well decide to cut the Gordian knot of the legality of congressional exclusion on the basis of whatever territorial legislation came before it. It is improbable that the Taney Court would have decided as it did, had not Congress already repealed the Missouri law in 1854. Congress had not renounced the power to exclude slavery in the territories, but it had renounced the exercise of that power.

Justice Roger B. Taney took the matter only one step further, confident that he was confirming what the president and Congress already had agreed should be done. He did not foresee any conflict between the Court and the elected branches and, indeed, *Dred Scott* was hailed by the Buchanan administration as well as by the leaders of the majority in both houses of Congress. Lincoln's "house divided" speech of 1858 contains the accusation of a political conspiracy to extend slavery among "Stephen, Franklin, Roger, and James"—that is, among Senator Douglas, Presidents Pierce and Buchanan, and Chief Justice Taney. Whether or not the collusion actually took place, Lincoln certainly was correct in seeing *Dred Scott* as the consequence of a political will far greater and more powerful than that of the Court by itself.

Dred Scott, moreover, did not contribute significantly to the coming of the Civil War because of its decision that Congress had no power to outlaw slavery in the territories. Far more deleterious were the consequences of Taney's obiter dictum concerning the power of Congress to guarantee slavery in the territories:

And no word can be found in the Constitution which gives Congress a greater power over slavery property [in the territories], or which entitles property of that kind to less protection than property of any other description. The only power conferred is the power coupled with the duty of guarding and protecting the owner in his rights.

Taney moved the sectional controversy on to a new plane by affirming that Congress possessed a constitutional duty to guard and protect the right of the owner of slaves to his slaves in the territories. Calhoun long ago had claimed "equality" between slave property and other property in the territories. Generally, this had been taken to refer to a right of ingress with slave property, rather than a right to federal—as distinct from territorial—protection, once the ingress had been achieved. Now, however, the proslavery radicals insisted upon the federal slave code to which Taney now told them they were entitled.

In May 1860 the representatives of the seven states of the Deep South "seceded" from the Democratic National Convention. This was the true origin of secession from the Union and the precipitating cause of the Civil War. The convention had shown a majority (but not two-thirds) preference for Stephen A. Douglas to be the Democratic candidate for president, but he and his supporters would not endorse the demand of the delegates of these seven states for a federal slave code. Douglas was committed to "popular sovereignty," to letting the settlers in the territories decide for themselves whether "to vote slavery up or vote slavery down." These delegates therefore bolted. As Don E. Fehrenbacher has said, "Everyone with eyes to see knew that those Southerners who would not accept Douglas as the presidential candidate of the Democratic party would never accept Lincoln as president of the United States." Thus, it was the promotion of the idea of a constitutional right to a federal slave code in the territories, rather than the denial of congressional power to exclude slavery from the territories, that made Taney's opinion in *Dred Scott* so deadly.

Meese contends that the issue in *Dred Scott* was not whether slavery was right or wrong but whether Congress had the power to keep it out of the territories. Whether one thought that Congress did or did not have such power depended upon whether one thought slavery right or wrong. That was the true state of the argument, from beginning to end, as Lincoln never ceased to insist. Writing as president-elect, in the midst of the secession crisis, to his old friend and former fellow Whig congressman—soon to become vice-president of the Confederacy—Alexander Stephens, Lincoln asked:

Do the people of the South really entertain fears that a Republican administration would, *directly* or *indirectly*, interfere with their slaves, or with them about their slaves? If they do, I wish to assure you, as once a friend, and still, I hope, not an enemy, that there is no cause for such fears.

The South would be in no more danger in this respect than it was in the days of Washington. I suppose, however, this does not meet the case. You think slavery is *right*, and ought to be extended; while we think it is *wrong* and ought to be restricted. That I suppose is the rub. It certainly is the only substantial difference between us. (Emphasis by Lincoln)

Taney had insisted that Congress had no power to exclude slavery from the territories because it had no power to discriminate between slave property or any other kind of property. Lincoln, arguing in 1854 against the repeal of the Missouri Compromise and long before *Dred Scott*, addressed this question with his classic argument:

Equal justice to the South, it is said, requires us to consent to the extending of slavery to new countries. That is to say, inasmuch as you do not object to my taking my hog to Nebraska, therefore I must not object to you taking your slave. Now, I admit this is perfectly logical, if there is no difference between hogs and negroes.

The doctrine of self-government is right—absolutely and eternally right—but it has no just application as here attempted—[namely, by Douglas in allowing the people in each territory to decide for themselves whether or not to have slavery]. Or perhaps I should say that whether it has such application depends upon whether a negro is *not* or *is* a man. If he is *not* a man, why in that case, he who *is* a man may, as a matter of self-government, do just as he pleases with him. But if the negro *is* a man, is it not to that extent a total destruction of self-government, to say that he too shall not govern *himself?* When the white man governs himself that is self-government; but when he governs himself, and also governs *another* man, that is more than self-government—that is despotism. If the negro is a *man*, why then my ancient faith teaches me that "all men are created equal," and that there can be no moral right in connection with one man's making a slave of another. (Emphasis by Lincoln)

The consitutional question of whether Congress had power over slavery in the territories depended upon whether Congress lawfully could draw a distinction between hogs and Negroes as chattel property.

Lincoln had pointed out that the same Southerners who insisted upon constitutional recognition of the "equality" between their slave property and the property of free state citizens—the equality of status between Negroes and hogs—never acted upon the assumption of any such equality in their own daily lives. There were no "free horses" or "free cattle" in these states. In fact, the objective reality of the difference between man and brute could not be obscured by the legal degradation of the Negro to the class of the brute. Reality, Lincoln insisted, must govern law. Law can only recognize reality, it cannot create it. In his speech, Lincoln showed that in many ways the Southern defenders of slavery acknowledged that reality. Certainly, they would never have pursued the comparison of Negro and hog to the point of permitting slaveowners to butcher, or to eat, the former. Indeed, their own laws treated Negro slaves as persons in many respects, both in providing them with at least some minimal security against unlawful violence and in making the slaves legally responsible for crimes against persons or property. In so doing they were treating the slaves not as chattels (that is, cattle) but as beings possessed of rational wills. This, however, meant that they too were "endowed by their Creator" with the unalienable rights proclaimed in the Declaration of Independence.

In his Peoria speech, Lincoln's argument against the constitutional "equality" of Negroes and hogs can be considered the greatest application of Socratic dialectic in deliberative rhetoric in the political addresses of the world. It is remarkable among Lincoln's speeches in that it does not start from the premises of the Declaration of Independence but appeals to universal human experience to show why doctrines of the Declaration are true. Lincoln demonstrates that a consistent human life is impossible if one denies the obligation of morality as between man and man. He argues that these obligations arise necessarily from our perceptions of what makes a human being human. We see that a human being, everywhere and always, is not a hog or a dog. We see that morality as the foundation of the rule of law follows inexorably from this perception. We see, in the final analysis, that our own self-respect and the respect in which we hold others are conditional upon recognizing and acting upon this fact. And we see that, in degrading others below the level of their humanity, we degrade ourselves below the level of our own. This, in the end, is self-defeating, since it is only in the light of our humanity that we can know and pursue the supreme human good: happiness.

The realization of the just regime, however, must proceed step by step; hence, the presence of slavery in the regime of the Founding Fathers. There is an old saying that it was far easier for Moses to get the Jews out of Egypt than it was for him to get Egypt out of the Jews. After all the Lord had done for their deliverance from bondage, as soon as Moses left them to themselves they began to worship the Golden Calf. Our own Founding Fathers knew that the idolatry of slavery was far too deeply rooted to be extirpated at once, and they would not arrogate to themselves the kind of authority that Moses exercised in the name of the Lord. The consent required by equality under the laws of nature forbade it.

The problem of founding a regime of freedom in a land of slavery can be best revealed in the following speech given by Calhoun in the Senate in 1847:

> I am a Southern man and a slaveholder—a kind and merciful one, I trust—and none the worse for being a slaveholder. I say, for one, I would rather meet any extremity upon earth than give up one inch of our equality—one inch of what belongs to us as members of this republic! What! acknowledged inferiority! The surrender of life is nothing to sinking down into acknowledged inferiority!

The "equality" which Calhoun claimed was not that of the Declaration of Independence. It was the constitutional equality of citizens of slave states with those of free states, defined as the equal right of the former with the latter, to enter territories of the United States with whatever property they might choose to bring with them. In short, it was equality defined as the right to treat Negroes as if they were hogs. Here Calhoun demonstrates how, and in what respect, he actually and literally does not recognize the difference between a human being and a brute. He speaks of himself as a kind and merciful slaveowner in just the same way he would speak of himself as a humane owner of dogs or horses. He speaks as one perfectly unconscious that the evil of "acknowledged inferiority" can be an evil for his slaves as for himself. He speaks as one unaware of their feelings as human beings, and in any event he denies that such feelings have any importance for morality, whether private or public. All this is implicit in his repudiation of the doctrine of the Declaration. Calhoun will not acknowledge any ground of equality, much as he claims it for himself as a citizen of the United States, in "the laws of nature and of nature's God." Thus do we see what may become of constitutional equality apart from its ground in natural equality. This, incidentally, is the current problem of interpreting the equal protection clause of the Fourteenth Amendment.

The inner crisis of American conservativism today is identical in principle with the crisis of the "house divided," the crisis of the Civil War. We must restore in our time, as Lincoln did in his, the interpretation of the Declaration of Independence as the key to the "original intentions" of those who drafted and those who ratified the Constitution. That restoration, however, will have to be accomplished in the teeth of the opposition of the Conservative intellectual establishment. The struggle will be long and hard. It is only hoped that the attorney general will not now flag or fail in carrying forward what he has begun.

1987...and the Next One Hundred Years

James MacGregor Burns

The Constitution is the most brilliant piece of political planning in the history of the Western world. To go back to the Founding Fathers, to look at their work, to read their correspondence, to know of their lives, to study the proceedings of the Constitutional Convention simply increases my absolute admiration for the genius of these thinkers and leaders. Even more, the Convention is the answer to those pessimists who say that human beings are so limited in creativity and vision that all we can hope to do is to make a little advance here and a little advance there, maybe step back and step to the side, and then push ahead. In one brilliant act of collective intellectual leadership, these men established a new political system, the results of which stare at us from the front page of practically every newspaper we read. There are literally thousands and thousands of examples of the constitutional system operating much as the Framers planned. The constitutional system, however, has serious failings and deficiencies in the face of what could be enormous pressures on us in the next one hundred or two hundred years.

What I will call the "second constitution" will be commemorated in 2000, the 200th anniversary of the year in which one party, the Federalists, yielded to their mortal enemies—the Jeffersonian Republicans—and came up with a marvelous idea: that in a democracy the majority tolerates the minority and allows that minority to take part in an election, win an election, and come into power. It was not easy; there was enormous tension in 1800. But the Federalists accomplished the mighty feat of letting the opposition party, a party of infidels and radicals headed by that dubious character, Thomas Jefferson, come into office.

This party system, the second constitution, is so called because it did and does much of what the Constitution did or does. Parties allot power, reserve power, distribute power, organize power, thereby controlling government and, in their own way, acting as do constitutions. The second constitution, however, is very much in contrast with the first Constitution. It was not established by a group of distinguished, rather elitist gentlemen meeting in Philadelphia; it was established in taverns, at crossroads, in legislatures, and in Congress. It originated in Congress, begun mainly by James Madison in the House, but then moved out to the people and was led later by Jefferson. By 1800 the country had an effective two-party system.

This second constitution, this party system, was founded not necessarily by proletarians but by plain people, by politicos, by tavernkeepers. I was reminded of the contributions of these plain people while doing some research. At the ratifying conventions following the Constitutional Convention, the Anti-Federalists—in their debates in the Massachusetts ratifying convention in Boston or the New York convention in Poughkeepsie or the Virginia convention in Richmond, with Patrick Henry and other great men—the grass-roots delegates proved the ability of the so-called common man to debate skillfully the difficult issues of the Constitution that had been framed the year before in Philadelphia. Although I usually urge people to study the background of their delegates, I learned a lesson myself in the dangers of doing so when I investigated the delegate from Williamstown, Massachusetts, to his state convention.

Williamstown then, as now, being a small community that boasts that it does not have even a single stoplight, did send a delegate to Boston. Looking him up, I discovered that he had been the local tavernkeeper. He then had become treasurer of Williams College. Next, this gentleman from Williamstown improbably was named treasurer of the Commonwealth of Massachusetts. At that point, he absconded with $55,000 from the state treasury. Therefore, when we talk about these plain people and other grass-roots leaders, compared to the virtuous men at Philadelphia, we are getting into areas of politics that sometimes yield dubious results.

In any event, that second constitution, the party constitution, thrived all during the nineteenth century. In that century a kind of rough and unstable equilibrium existed between the first Constitution that fragmented and divided power and the second, or party, constitution that brought power together. The parties unified government not because they were virtuous but because they wanted to obtain power. They also desired to implement their programs. By banding together they could win elections, and, if they won office, they could run the government. This was the party system, the second constitution. It was government by majority rule, compared to the first

Constitution, which was hostile to the concept of majority rule. The second constitution did not work perfectly, any more than did the first one, but it brought about a great broadening of democracy in this country and the extension of suffrage. By the end of the century, aside from the fact that most women still were not able to vote and many blacks had never been able to vote, the party system, to a considerable extent, had democratized a Constitution deliberately made undemocratic, or at least antimajoritarian by the Framers.

At the start of the century following that period of equilibrium between the two constitutions, one of them collapsed. If this had been France, it would have been the formal, written constitution, since France likes to experiment with different ones. But this was America, then a country filled with virtuous reformers who did not like many aspects of the party system. Many of our forefathers in California were members of that great Progressive movement because California took the lead in the destruction of the second constitution. It took the lead in the destruction, or certainly the undermining, of the party system in this country by adopting laws that limited good party politicians from going about their daily rounds of patronage and perhaps a little election rigging and corruption. But it also teamed up to make government work. At the same time, this movement throttled the democratic impulse of the party system.

California passed practically all the reforms that were damaging to the party system; states like Wisconsin did the same. Other states, in the early part of this century and thereafter, have been cutting out the very heart of the party system by taking from the party its most crucial function, the nominating function. The only real distinction about political parties is the power to nominate; otherwise, they become just another of Madison's factions. Parties put names on the ballot, a crucial function, as anyone knows who has ever tried for political office.

That happy equilibrium, therefore, which on the whole had been a rather fruitful, productive, and effective system, no longer existed in its old form. One of the impressive aspects of the equilibrium between the two constitutions had been the capacity of the parties to govern when they were needed to govern. For example, following the Civil War the Republican party took on the job of Reconstruction. It did not do so good a job as it should have, but for a while we had an experiment in "naked majority rule," much to the horror and outrage of the Southerners. And, for a few years, the Republicans conducted an experiment in putting through a program forged before and during the Civil War, not only to emancipate black men and women but also to try to give them a chance in life. That experiment largely failed, but at least an effort was made that otherwise would not have been undertaken at all. Indeed, the Civil War itself was an indictment of the constitutional system that could not deal with the intensity of that conflict. Thus, that kind of balance between the two constitutions was lost.

Now there was no longer a party system that could move during the crises of the twentieth century to strengthen government, to link the branches together, and to make it a more effective instrument in dealing with those crises. It is in part because of the decline of that effective party system that we today have a low-voltage political system: the extent of nonvoting; the fact that almost one-half the citizens do not take part in our "game" of democracy; the general loss of confidence in political institutions in this country; and, above all, the absence of what is perhaps the most crucial value in the mechanics of democracy, that of responsibility, accountability, the capacity of people to put their finger on who should get credit or discredit for what has happened in government.

Our elections are not decisive tests of leadership. Election campaigns tend to be a vast game of finger pointing as each side blames the other. Since every party and every faction have had a hand in what has been done, it is easy to shrug off responsibility onto other parties and other factions. Although I do not believe that we should try to import the parliamentary system, I admire that aspect of the British way that makes it possible for their electorate in a general election to know just who has been responsible for whatever good or bad has happened since the last election. When Margaret Thatcher and her party's M.P. candidates go back before the electorate, they will not be able to shrug off responsibility or blame the Opposition, because the Opposition has not had the power. The Opposition has done its job of opposing. Since the government has had the power, it stands accountable for that power. The concept of responsibility is at the very heart of democracy. That is what an effective party system and an effective opposition party bring about, but this is very hard to achieve under a Constitution that divides up power as skillfully as does our system.

Why, then, beyond this problem of responsibility do I take a critical view of the effectiveness of our Constitution today? Aside from the issue of responsibility, I am most disturbed by the way we have not only undermined the second constitution but also in certain ways undermined the first. Governments have to deal with crises. If the person in office fails to handle a crisis efficiently, such as Herbert Hoover did, then he yields in an election to someone who can deal better with crisis—in that case Franklin D. Roosevelt. If government does not respond and if human needs are not met, or if crisis situations are not dealt with, people will demand action on the part of their governors.

However, what happens when the constitutional system inhibits action? In the United States, in this century particularly, we have worked out the most marvelous and dubious method of evading the delays and compromises implicit in the constitutional checks and balances. We have used what Arthur Schlesinger so aptly has called the imperial presidency. We have, in effect, dumped power into the hands of the president, not so much because he has wanted it but because we have wanted him to have it. We have built up an arsenal of presidential powers. Practically no one seems to question a president who takes warlike actions today, except when things go wrong, and then there is a tremendous reaction when it is too late to remedy the situation.

Aside from the president's war-making power—still extensive despite the War Powers Act—executive agreements are a way for presidents to get around the Senate's two-thirds treaty requirement. One rather hesitates to denounce presidents who may think that they have majority support in the Senate for a treaty but fear putting a treaty before that body which runs the risk of not gaining a two-thirds vote. Presidents may see this as an impossible hurdle. Thus, they have won the power to make with other nations executive agreements that have the force of law.

Therefore, why should a president take his chances in the Senate with its two-thirds rule if by the stroke of a pen he can, in effect, make a treaty with another nation? In some respects, we are not even honest; we are not even adhering to the implications of our old-fashioned Constitution. We are finding ways to evade the checks and balances and yet, when it comes to mobilizing governmental power to anticipate problems, to head problems off—as, for example, to pass a child labor amendment (which was never passed in this country and which took decades before it was even passed in a somewhat disguised fashion in the Wages and Hours Act of 1938)—government fails to act. Those who believe in the first Constitution say that it may take a little longer, but finally we will do it. It is not so easy, however, for those who will spend a lifetime working twelve hours per day as children and as adults; a whole generation can be lost. In any event, it is the ability in crisis times to turn to that cheap and dangerous weapon of presidential emergency power that also makes us less effective in planning ahead and mobilizing governmental, economic, and other powers—human power—to deal with the tremendous problems of the modern world.

Therefore, we should go back to the second constitution and not impair our first Constitution. As for the first, we should keep many of its great features, most notably the Bill of Rights. To the extent that the first Constitution radically disperses power and makes it impossible for government to operate as a collective agency, we should reestablish the second constitution, reestablish and democratize our party system.

Strengthening the party system calls for action in many states that would be too tedious to enumerate here. But, at the very least, we should do something about the hideous cost of campaigning and about developing a whole level of party democracy beneath the rather old-fashioned precinct and ward committees. We also should encourage party democracy, party issue building, and party network building as a way to strengthen the party system from the bottom as well as from the top.

On the side of strengthening the Constitution, we might first consider strengthening the impeachment power. Today that power is very limited—for malfeasance in office, for example. But what about cases where presidents hopelessly have lost the confidence of the people, or where there is the potential for a presidential crisis? Should we not have some capacity to deal with horrendous presidential situations? I am not talking about simply disagreeing with the president, but about situations where the safety of the Republic and the leadership of the nation are gravely imperiled by some presidential action or situation.

Second, we might make a modest reform in our electoral system. One of its most obvious weaknesses is the two-year term for congressmen. Representatives must start raising money and electioneering for their next term before they even have a chance to settle down in Washington. Also, the midterm election is another weakness. A really low-voltage election, it tends to be localistic in character and almost always to go against a president no matter how well he may have done. It makes it almost impossible for a team of people elected in a presidential year to establish a record to present in the next election, for either a vote of support or of disavowal.

A third proposal is that we experiment with the so-called legislative-executive cabinet or, to put it more simply, that we permit the president, under the Constitution as changed, to select members of Congress for his cabinet without requiring them to give up their congressional seats. Today he can select members of Congress, but they cannot hold both jobs at once. It is doubtful that presidents would want to select sitting congressmen, but I can imagine a situation in which there is an exceptionally able chairman of the Foreign Relations Committee, or the equivalent in the House. It would be a strengthening factor in a presidential cabinet to have such members of Congress bring to the cabinet their experience and contacts and, at the same time, take back to Congress the benefit of that experience close to the presidency. This arrangement is typical in parliamentary systems, and it is one aspect of the parliamentary way we might want to consider.

Finally, I would like to recommend the "team ticket," an old-fashioned device that flourished under the second constitution. This allowed a voter who might not know very much about the candidates—say, an immigrant who only knew that, for him, the Democratic party catered to his needs, or a young businessman who did not know much about politics but thought that the Republican party was the party of Horatio Alger—simply to look for the "D" or the "R" and vote for a whole ticket under either of those labels. That is, candidates were lined up on the ballot by party, and it was possible in some states to vote for the whole party ticket with one check or with one move of the lever.

This device was attacked by reformers who wanted voters to be able to pick and choose. We lost something, however, when we eliminated that kind of direct support of political teamwork on the part of people who could make some distinction, at least between Democrats and Republicans. Some years ago I remember researching not only public opinion data but also the sort of "chaff" that went along with it and finding what people would answer when they were being polled. One woman said that she did not know much about politics, but she "liked them Democrats because they shelled out the money" when they were in power. That remark makes any good Republican blanch, but the woman had caught on to a vital aspect of American politics: the Democrats like to spend money for human welfare, and the Republicans tend not to. If she knew that, she knew something related to her particular needs. I would like to see an electoral system that makes that kind of voting possible.

In conclusion, constitutions, whether the first or the second, are written for decades, or should be. Having little ability to foresee the future, I tried putting myself in the position of commencement orators over fifty-year periods, going back in time from the present. Would any of those commencement orators, although terribly pessimistic, have predicted what would be happening in this country during the following fifty years in order to prepare students for the years ahead? No one could have predicted the Revolution. Who could have predicted the Civil War twenty or thirty years in advance, or Reconstruction, or the savage impact of the Industrial Revolution? Who could have predicted two world wars in the twentieth century, or the Holocaust, or the nuclear bomb? In every case, I would have failed to give a sense of the dire impact of what lay ahead for those people who might live into the next fifty years.

Could anyone now look into the next fifty or one hundred or two hundred years and not share the feeling that the passions of the world are loose? We cannot escape them, as we have been discovering throughout this century. Thus, if we are really to honor what the Framers did, we must be willing to do what they did: to stand back from the existing political system, look at it in terms of future possibilities, think daringly, and act daringly as we try to put our constitutional house in order.

Commentary to James MacGregor Burns

Robert Dawidoff

The Constitution is like an old machine, one that requires more ingenuity than we can sometimes muster to keep it working right, one whose creaks and groans and expense have multiplied with age into a rather constant roar and drain. Is it worth the upkeep, or might not a new machine be a prudent investment? My retro sensibility says that there is something seemly and beautiful in the workings of the old Constitution, something of an argument for it in its very longevity. The difference, though, between the retro and the merely nostalgic or the reactionary is a critical one. Retro man believes that knowledge is power and has reasons for his beliefs. If something new serves a better purpose or looks better than something old, put the old in a museum and use the new. However, the Constitution works quite well, as well as governments ever work.

Although every effort must be made to render government more effective, it is still somewhat haphazard in what it can achieve. It is wise to take care of ourselves as if there were a complete correlation between good care and long life, but there is only a limited correlation, with so much in life dependent on unforeseen events. The human condition is what governments, like people, have to struggle with daily. The Founders believed in both human effort and the human condition.

The Constitution promotes national energy without depending on an unrealistic view of human nature or the human condition. At any moment in national life the Constitution encourages improvement and, at the same time, discourages too many sacrifices of basic goods, like liberty, in the name of even the most pressing emergencies. If the Declaration of Independence—what Robert Frost called that hard mystery of Jefferson's—keeps us on our toes, looking toward the future, giving our national life an ideal, then the Constitution puts the brake on our reaching. Although in some circumstances a doctrine of national unity, the Constitution is grounded in contrary effort. It offers an instant critique of any moment.

The Constitution is at its most characteristic when some present course of action is slowed or stymied or compromised, even ruined. If the Declaration is the child in the body politic, then the Constitution was always prematurely gray. Its secret motto concerns the best-laid plans. It was written in the cynical conviction that power corrupts, and that the best way to limit inevitable corruption was to confuse, that is, divide the power.

The greatest calls for national unity, in wartime and peacetime, have tended to be unconstitutional or extraconstitutional. Lacunae in the Constitution seem to provide for its occasional supercession and circumvention, for the evolution around it of a political culture, but the document itself invokes no emotion, just process. It has been used by those who have wanted to change it, and each generation has taken sides over its contrary tendencies, a view that has always defined, and usually safely divided, American politics. Our history records the political lives Americans have given to the Constitution's bare bones.

One of the great lessons of constitutional history is to see the various phases of our constitutional remodeling. There was that fantastic leap under the first stress of nationhood when not only the Marshall Court but also the Jeffersonians themselves strained an order keeping federal compact to national purposes. Judicial review was no more expansive a reading of the Constitution than the Louisiana Purchase, after all, with much the same result. The 1930s put a kind of Art Deco streamlining pressure on the Constitution, one with which we are still coping. Who would have thought that the very issues our Founders believed the Constitution might buffer—the issues of world empire and religion and private morality that they figured had ruined every body politic—now would be chief among the constitutional issues before all three branches of our government?

The Founders knew very well that the division of power would lead to stalemate and quarrel. They were all experienced, political men whose desire for a national energy was not freed from a genuine worry about national energy. We are far enough away from their antidemocratic suspiciousness to recognize that the particular *who* they feared, in their case the Beast people, is less important than their suspicion that some *who* or other would always be a menace to freedom and tranquility. The political passions and interests of the moment, whoever they are and whatever they might be, are what the Constitution seeks not to deny but to delay. In what the Founders set up, national energy continually is exposed to a series of institutional checks and balances, to roadblocks—often procedural, often personal, often corrupt, and often stupid.

The Founders seemed to have had too firm a grasp of the unhappy variety of human types and what they regarded as the worrisome tendency of human nature to put their faith in men as they were, let alone to plan as if they were angels. They did not regard the prospect of national life as likely to improve human nature, or even to redeem it. Thus, they trusted liberty and union to a kind of orderly confusion.

It is reassuring to know that something in the very nature of our regime makes it susceptible to petty delay. The mustered forces of right may not be able to persuade a president, but the self-interest of a congressman and his sense of pork-barrel reality can hamper the war powers of the executive in the nuclear age. One cannot always admire the way this works, but it does seem suited to the modern world in which the random seems to play such a large part, in which compromise seems both more fleeting and necessary than ever before, and in which recognizable human motive and personality seem to be disappearing in public life.

The doctrine of self-interest that goes along with an eternal skepticism of power, while not the most flattering to human self-consequence, is a good one in a world where power battens on flattery and where self-interest and self-consequence have become almost synonymous. Maybe the Constitution is realistic about human beings, maybe living under it for two hundred years has made Americans into the people it infers, but it seems to be instead a system under which life is comparatively human-scaled. Since it is exactly this human element of life that I see imperiled in the next one hundred years, it is the lifelike quality of our Constitution that provides the most interesting resource for the future.

Originating in an age when the best wisdom was skeptical about power and people and valued minority rights, by which the Founders likely meant property, but which they identified differently in the first Ten Amendments, the Constitution possesses an earthbound sense of government. Religion was a private sanction in those days, and the document tries to maintain it that way. In its inherent patriotic sensibility, the Constitution leaves patriotism to the imagination and to the individual. Even in this age of petulant and self-deceiving imperial self-celebration, our Constitution protects us in the proper objects of patriotic desire and is a lesson in public propriety.

Finally, at its core, unlike our national culture, which it seems to have influenced very little, the Constitution is a limited and limiting document. Every American is an adherent of the Declaration, but the Constitution has few followers and precious few readers. The deepest contemporary dissatisfactions with the Constitution have been about how far it will, or should, stretch to cover the unforeseen. It will stretch only so far without revealing those who are trying to stretch it.

In making more effective the Declaration's exaggerated promise of American life, the Constitution does not take the place of "We the People"; it depends on every level of political participation. This understanding that human government is only as good or as bad as the human beings exercising limited, balanced, and contrary powers at any given time is the great persisting fact about our Constitution. Under our system we can only delude ourselves. The inefficiency and the incapacity for streamlined, split-second decision making inherent in our system are almost the last stand of the view of human nature held by the Founders, profoundly suspicious and also profoundly real, that people are capable of free government because they are held responsible for it.

The worst I imagine about the next one hundred years, barring nuclear catastrophe, is the increasing corruption of individual human lives by the centralizing deceptive forces of our common corporate culture, both media-enforced and media-simulated; the kinds of people who make up We the People seem beguiled by the bloated images of themselves thrown up on six-foot screens. This situation might benefit, however, from the views that informed the Constitution. These views are little adhered to now, preferring reason to faith, individual to agglomerate, private to public; skeptical of power, interested in compromise, diffident about display, leery of empire; historical, philosophical, democratic (yes, democratic), hopeful but not necessarily optimistic, realistic and idealistic—the Constitution steeps us in a serious view of the human condition, which is more than American culture does right now.

To keep us company, then, in the next one hundred years are the wearying and sometimes deadlocking reminders of the human condition as our Founders saw it. Our luck in the Constitution is that its critique of the present moment comes from the American Enlightenment. The workings of the Constitution lend to our present what was a historical moment of unusual quality. However shadowy its effect at times appears, that shadow is worth trying to cast. Not only enlightened, the Founders also had been stirred to political action, for good or ill, disappointed in their first try at nationhood and inspired by that experience to try again to make their best hopes work. Their experience is still, as Douglass Adair has reminded us, our only guide.

Both Abe Lincoln and Jack Teagarden passed withering judgments on the importance of any present moment in the light of the next one hundred years, and anything those two agreed on must be so. There is no magic in the Constitution for what is bound to be its third troubled century; it did not exactly hold answers to the last two. Retro man merely notes that the tension between the Declaration and the Constitution remains a real life-describing tension. We really can live a life trying to figure out Jefferson's hard mystery, wandering in Madison's curious maze.

Appendixes

The Declaration of Independence

In Congress, July 4, 1776:
The Unanimous Declaration of
the Thirteen United States of America

When in the Course of human events, it becomes necessary for one people to dissolve the political bands which have connected them with another, and to assume among the Powers of the earth, the separate and equal station to which the Laws of Nature and of Nature's God entitle them, a decent respect to the opinions of mankind requires that they should declare the causes which impel them to the separation.

We hold these truths to be self-evident, that all men are created equal, that they are endowed by their Creator with certain unalienable Rights, that among these are Life, Liberty and the pursuit of Happiness. That to secure these rights, Governments are instituted among Men, deriving their just powers from the consent of the governed, That whenever any Form of Government becomes destructive of these ends, it is the Right of the People to alter or to abolish it, and to institute new Government, laying its foundation on such principles and organizing its powers in such form, as to them shall seem most likely to effect their Safety and Happiness. Prudence, indeed, will dictate that Governments long established should not be changed for light and transient causes; and accordingly all experience hath shown, that mankind are more disposed to suffer, while evils are sufferable, than to right themselves by abolishing the forms to which they are accustomed. But when a long train of abuses and usurpations, pursuing invariably the same Object evinces a design to reduce them under absolute Despotism, it is their right, it is their duty, to throw off such Government, and to provide new Guards for their future security—Such has been the patient sufferance of these Colonies; and such is now the necessity which constrains them to alter their former Systems of Government. The history of the present

King of Great Britain is a history of repeated injuries and usurpations, all having in direct object the establishment of an absolute Tyranny over these States. To prove this, let Facts be submitted to a candid world.

He has refused his Assent to Laws, the most wholesome and necessary for the public good.

He has forbidden his Governors to pass Laws of immediate and pressing importance, unless suspended in their operation till his Assent should be obtained; and when so suspended, he has utterly neglected to attend to them.

He has refused to pass other Laws for the accommodation of large districts of people, unless those people would relinquish the right of representation in the Legislature, a right inestimable to them and formidable to tyrants only.

He has called together legislative bodies at places unusual, uncomfortable, and distant from the depository of their Public Records, for the sole purpose of fatiguing them into compliance with his measures.

He has dissolved Representative Houses repeatedly, for opposing with manly firmness his invasions on the rights of the people.

He has refused for a long time, after such dissolutions, to cause others to be elected; whereby the Legislative Powers, incapable of Annihilation, have returned to the People at large for their exercise; the State remaining in the mean time exposed to all the dangers of invasion from without, and convulsions within.

He has endeavoured to prevent the population of these States; for that purpose obstructing the Laws of Naturalization of Foreigners; refusing to pass others to encourage their migrations hither, and raising the conditions of new Appropriations of Lands.

He has obstructed the Administration of Justice, by refusing his Assent to Laws for establishing Judiciary Powers.

He has made Judges dependent on his Will alone, for the tenure of their offices, and the amount and payment of their salaries.

He has erected a multitude of New Offices, and sent hither swarms of Officers to harass our People, and eat out their substance.

He has kept among us, in times of peace, Standing Armies without the Consent of our legislatures.

He has affected to render the Military independent of and superior to the Civil Power.

He has combined with others to subject us to a jurisdiction foreign to our constitution, and unacknowledged by our laws; giving his Assent to their acts of pretended legislation:

For quartering large bodies of armed troops among us:

For protecting them, by a mock Trial, from Punishment for any Murders which they should commit on the Inhabitants of these States:

For cutting off our Trade with all parts of the world:

For imposing taxes on us without our Consent:

For depriving us in many cases, of the benefits of Trial by jury:

For transporting us beyond Seas to be tried for pretended offences:

For abolishing the free System of English Laws in a neighboring Province, establishing therein an Arbitrary government, and enlarging its Boundaries so as to render it at once an example and fit instrument for introducing the same absolute rule into these Colonies:

For taking away our Charters, abolishing our most valuable Laws, and altering fundamentally the Forms of our Governments:

For suspending our own legislatures, and declaring themselves invested with Power to legislate for us in all cases whatsoever.

He has abdicated Government here, by declaring us out of his Protection and waging War against us.

He has plundered our seas, ravaged our Coasts, burnt our towns, and destroyed the lives of our people.

He is at this time transporting large armies of foreign mercenaries to compleat the works of death, desolation and tyranny, already begun with circumstances of Cruelty & perfidy scarcely paralleled in the most barbarous ages, and totally unworthy the Head of a civilized nation.

He has constrained our fellow Citizens taken Captive on the high Seas to bear Arms against their Country, to become the executioners of their friends and Brethren, or to fall themselves by their Hands.

He has excited domestic insurrections amongst us, and has endeavoured to bring on the inhabitants of our frontiers, the merciless Indian Savages, whose known rule of warfare, is an undistinguished destruction of all ages, sexes and conditions.

In every stage of these Oppressions We have Petitioned for Redress in the most humble terms: Our repeated Petitions have been answered only by repeated injury. A Prince, whose character is thus marked by every act which may define a Tyrant, is unfit to be the ruler of a free People.

Nor have We been wanting in attentions to our British brethren. We have warned them from time to time of attempts by their legislature to extend an unwarrantable jurisdiction over us. We have reminded them of the circumstances of our emigration and settlement here. We have appealed to their native justice and magnanimity, and we have conjured them by the ties of our common kindred to disavow these usurpations, which would inevitably interrupt our connections and correspondence. They too have been deaf to the voice of justice and of consanguinity. We must, therefore, acquiesce in the necessity, which denounces our Separation, and hold them, as we hold the rest of mankind, Enemies in War, in Peace Friends.

We, therefore, the Representatives of the United States of America, in General Congress, Assembled, appealing to the Supreme Judge of the world for the rectitude of our intentions, do, in the Name, and by Authority of the good People of these Colonies, solemnly publish and declare, That these United Colonies are, and of Right ought to be Free and Independent States; that they are Absolved from all Allegiance to the British Crown and that all political connection between them and the State of Great Britain, is and ought to be totally dissolved; and that as Free and Independent states, they have full Power to levy War, conclude Peace, contract Alliances, establish Commerce, and to do all other Acts and Things which Independent States may of right do. And for the support of this Declaration, with a firm reliance on the Protection of Divine Providence, we mutually pledge to each other our Lives, our Fortunes and our sacred Honor.

JOHN HANCOCK*

*The remaining signatures are omitted.

The Constitution of the United States

We the People of the United States, in order to form a more perfect union, establish justice, insure domestic tranquility, provide for the common defense, promote the general welfare, and secure the blessings of liberty to ourselves and our posterity, do ordain and establish this Constitution for the United States of America.

Article I

Section 1

All legislative powers herein granted shall be vested in a Congress of the United States, which shall consist of a Senate and House of Representatives.

Section 2

1. The House of Representatives shall be composed of members chosen every second year by the people of the several States, and the electors in each State shall have the qualifications requisite for electors of the most numerous branch of the State legislature.

2. No person shall be a representative who shall not have attained to the age of twenty-five years, and been seven years a citizen of the United States, and who shall not, when elected, be an inhabitant of that State in which he shall be chosen.

3. Representatives and direct taxes[1] shall be apportioned among the several States which may be included within this Union, according to their respective numbers, which shall be determined by adding to the whole number of free persons, including those bound to service for a term of years, and excluding Indians not taxed, three-fifths of all other persons.[2] The actual enumeration shall be made within three years after the first meeting of the Congress of the United States, and within every subsequent term of ten years, in such

---

[1]See the Sixteenth Amendment.
[2]Partly superseded by the Fourteenth Amendment.

manner as they shall by law direct. The number of representatives shall not exceed one for every thirty thousand, but each State shall have at least one representative; and until such enumeration shall be made, the State of New Hampshire shall be entitled to choose three, Massachusetts eight, Rhode Island and Providence Plantations one, Connecticut five, New York six, New Jersey four, Pennsylvania eight, Delaware one, Maryland six, Virginia ten, North Carolina five, South Carolina five, and Georgia three.

4. When vacancies happen in the representation from any State, the executive authority thereof shall issue writs of election to fill such vacancies.

5. The House of Representatives shall choose their speaker and other officers; and shall have the sole power of impeachment.

Section 3

1. The Senate of the United States shall be composed of two senators from each State, chosen by the legislature thereof,[3] for six years; and each senator shall have one vote.

2. Immediately after they shall be assembled in consequence of the first election, they shall be divided as equally as may be into three classes. The seats of the senators of the first class shall be vacated at the expiration of the second year, of the second class at the expiration of the fourth year, and of the third class at the expiration of the sixth year, so that one-third may be chosen every second year; and if vacancies happen by resignation, or otherwise, during the recess of the legislature of any State, the executive thereof may make temporary appointments until the next meeting of the legislature, which shall then fill such vacancies.[4]

3. No person shall be a senator who shall not have attained to the age of thirty years, and been nine years a citizen of the United States, and who shall not, when elected, be an inhabitant of that State for which he shall be chosen.

4. The Vice President of the United States shall be President of the Senate, but shall have no vote, unless they be equally divided.

5. The Senate shall choose their other officers, and also a president *pro tempore,* in the absence of the Vice President, or when he shall exercise the office of President of the United States.

6. The Senate shall have the sole power to try all impeachments. When sitting for that purpose, they shall be on oath or affirmation.

[3]See the Seventeenth Amendment.
[4]Ibid.

When the President of the United States is tried, the chief justice shall preside: and no person shall be convicted without the concurrence of two-thirds of the members present.

7. Judgment in cases of impeachment shall not extend further than to removal from office, and disqualification to hold and enjoy any office of honor, trust or profit under the United States: but the party convicted shall nevertheless be liable and subject to indictment, trial, judgment and punishment, according to law.

Section 4

1. The times, places, and manner of holding elections for senators and representatives, shall be prescribed in each State by the legislature thereof; but the Congress may at any time by law make or alter such regulations, except as to the places of choosing senators.

2. The Congress shall assemble at least once in every year, and such meeting shall be on the first Monday in December, unless they shall by law appoint a different day.

Section 5

1. Each House shall be the judge of the elections, returns and qualifications of its own members, and a majority of each shall constitute a quorum to do business; but a smaller number may adjourn from day to day, and may be authorized to compel the attendance of absent members, in such manner and under such penalties as each House may provide.

2. Each House may determine the rules of its proceedings, punish its members for disorderly behavior, and, with the concurrence of two-thirds, expel a member.

3. Each House shall keep a journal of its proceedings, and from time to time publish the same, excepting such parts as may in their judgment require secrecy; and the yeas and nays of the members of either House on any question shall, at the desire of one-fifth of those present, be entered on the journal.

4. Neither House, during the session of Congress, shall, without the consent of the other, adjourn for more than three days, nor to any other place than that in which the two Houses shall be sitting.

Section 6

1. The senators and representatives shall receive a compensation for their services, to be ascertained by law, and paid out of the

Treasury of the United States. They shall in all cases, except treason, felony and breach of the peace, be privileged from arrest during their attendance at the session of their respective Houses, and in going to and returning from the same; and for any speech or debate in either House, they shall not be questioned in any other place.

2. No senator or representative shall, during the time for which he was elected, be appointed to any civil office under the authority of the United States, which shall have been created, or the emoluments whereof shall have been increased during such time, and no person holding any office under the United States shall be a member of either House during his continuance in office.

Section 7

1. All bills for raising revenue shall originate in the House of Representatives; but the Senate may propose or concur with amendments as on other bills.

2. Every bill which shall have passed the House of Representatives and the Senate, shall, before it become a law, be presented to the President of the United States; if he approve he shall sign it, but if not he shall return it, with his objections to that House in which it shall have originated, who shall enter the objections at large on their journal, and proceed to reconsider it. If after such reconsideration two thirds of that House shall agree to pass the bill, it shall be sent, together with the objections, to the other House, by which it shall likewise be reconsidered, and if approved by two thirds of that House, it shall become a law. But in all such cases the votes of both Houses shall be determined by yeas and nays, and the names of the persons voting for and against the bill shall be entered on the journal of each House respectively. If any bill shall not be returned by the President within ten days (Sundays excepted) after it shall have been presented to him, the same shall be a law, in like manner as if he had signed it, unless the Congress by their adjournment prevent its return, in which case it shall not be a law.

3. Every order, resolution, or vote to which the concurrence of the Senate and House of Representatives may be necessary (except on a question of adjournment) shall be presented to the President of the United States; and before the same shall take effect, shall be approved by him, or being disapproved by him, shall be repassed by two thirds of the Senate and House of Representatives, according to the rules and limitations prescribed in the case of a bill.

Section 8

1. The Congress shall have power:

To lay and collect taxes, duties, imposts, and excises, to pay the debts and provide for the common defence and general welfare of the United States; but all duties, imposts, and excises shall be uniform throughout the United States;

2. To borrow money on the credit of the United States;

3. To regulate commerce with foreign nations, and among the several States, and with the Indian tribes;

4. To establish an uniform rule of naturalization, and uniform laws on the subject of bankruptcies throughout the United States;

5. To coin money, regulate the value thereof, and of foreign coin, and fix the standard of weights and measures;

6. To provide for the punishment of counterfeiting the securities and current coin of the United States;

7. To establish post offices and post roads;

8. To promote the progress of science and useful arts, by securing for limited times to authors and inventors the exclusive right to their respective writings and discoveries;

9. To constitute tribunals inferior to the Supreme Court;

10. To define and punish piracies and felonies committed on the high seas, and offences against the law of nations;

11. To declare war, grant letters of marque and reprisal, and make rules concerning captures on land and water;

12. To raise and support armies, but no appropriation of money to that use shall be for a longer term than two years;

13. To provide and maintain a navy;

14. To make rules for the government and regulation of the land and naval forces;

15. To provide for calling forth the militia to execute the laws of the Union, suppress insurrections and repel invasions;

16. To provide for organizing, arming, and disciplining the militia, and for governing such part of them as may be employed in the service of the United States, reserving to the States respectively the appointment of the officers, and the authority of training the militia according to the discipline prescribed by Congress;

17. To exercise exclusive legislation in all cases whatsoever, over such district (not exceeding ten miles square) as may, by cession of particular States, and the acceptance of Congress, become the seat of the government of the United States, and to exercise like authority over all places purchased by the consent of the legislature of the

State in which the same shall be, for the erection of forts, magazines, dockyards, and other needful buildings; and

18. To make all laws which shall be necessary and proper for carrying into execution the foregoing powers, and all other powers vested by this Constitution in the government of the United States, or in any department or officer thereof.

Section 9

1. The migration or importation of such persons as any of the States now existing shall think proper to admit, shall not be prohibited by the Congress prior to the year one thousand eight hundred and eight, but a tax or duty may be imposed on such importation, not exceeding ten dollars for each person.

2. The privilege of the writ of *habeas corpus* shall not be suspended, unless when in cases of rebellion or invasion the public safety may require it.

3. No bill of attainder or *ex post facto* law shall be passed.

4. No capitation, or other direct, tax shall be laid, unless in proportion to the census or enumeration herein before directed to be taken.[5]

5. No tax or duty shall be laid on articles exported from any State.

6. No preference shall be given by any regulation of commerce or revenue to the ports of one State over those of another: nor shall vessels bound to, or from, one State be obliged to enter, clear, or pay duties in another.

7. No money shall be drawn from the Treasury, but in consequence of appropriations, made by law; and a regular statement and account of the receipts and expenditures of all public money shall be published from time to time.

8. No title of nobility shall be granted by the United States: and no person holding any office of profit or trust under them, shall, without the consent of the Congress, accept of any present, emolument, office, or title, of any kind whatever, from any king, prince, or foreign State.

Section 10

1. No State shall enter into any treaty, alliance, or confederation; grant letters of marque and reprisal; coin money; emit bills of credit; make anything but gold and silver coin a tender in payment

[5]See the Sixteenth Amendment.

of debts; pass any bill of attainder, *ex post facto* law, or law impairing the obligation of contracts, or grant any title of nobility.

2. No State shall, without the consent of the Congress, lay any imposts or duties on imports or exports, except what may be absolutely necessary for executing its inspection laws: and the net produce of all duties and imposts laid by any State on imports or exports, shall be for the use of the Treasury of the United States; and all such laws shall be subject to the revision and control of the Congress.

3. No State shall, without the consent of Congress, lay any duty of tonnage, keep troops, or ships of war in time of peace, enter into any agreement or compact with another State, or with a foreign power, or engage in war, unless actually invaded, or in such imminent danger as will not admit of delay.

Article II

Section 1

1. The executive power shall be vested in a President of the United States of America. He shall hold his office during the term of four years, and, together with the Vice President, chosen for the same term, be elected, as follows:[6]

2. Each State shall appoint, in such manner as the legislature thereof may direct, a number of electors, equal to the whole number of senators and representatives to which the State may be entitled in the Congress: but no senator or representative, or person holding an office of trust or profit under the United States, shall be appointed an elector.

The electors shall meet in their respective States, and vote by ballot for two persons, of whom one at least shall not be an inhabitant of the same State with themselves. And they shall make a list of all the persons voted for, and of the number of votes for each; which list they shall sign and certify, and transmit sealed to the seat of the government of the United States, directed to the president of the Senate. The president of the Senate shall, in the presence of the Senate and House of Representatives, open all the certificates, and the votes shall then be counted. The person having the greatest number of votes shall be the President, if such number be a majority of the whole number of electors appointed; and if there be more than one who have such majority, and have an equal number of votes, then the House of Representatives shall immediately choose by ballot one of them for President; and if no person have a majority, then from the five highest on the list the said House shall in like

[6]See the Twenty-second Amendment.

manner choose the President. But in choosing the President, the votes shall be taken by States, the representation from each State having one vote; a quorum for this purpose shall consist of a member or members from two thirds of the States, and a majority of all the States shall be necessary to a choice. In every case, after the choice of the President, the person having the greatest number of votes of the electors shall be the Vice President. But if there should remain two or more who have equal votes, the Senate shall choose from them by ballot the Vice President.[7]

3. The Congress may determine the time of choosing the electors, and the day on which they shall give their votes; which day shall be the same throughout the United States.

4. No person except a natural born citizen, or a citizen of the United States, at the time of the adoption of this Constitution, shall be eligible to the office of President; neither shall any person be eligible to that office who shall not have attained to the age of thirty-five years, and been fourteen years a resident within the United States.

5. In case of the removal of the President from office, or of his death, resignation, or inability to discharge the powers and duties of the said office, the same shall devolve on the Vice President, and the Congress may by law provide for the case of removal, death, resignation, or inability, both of the President and Vice President, declaring what officer shall then act as President, and such officer shall act accordingly, until the disability be removed, or a President shall be elected.[8]

6. The President shall, at stated times, receive for his services a compensation, which shall neither be increased nor diminished during the period for which he shall have been elected, and he shall not receive within that period any other emolument from the United States, or any of them.

7. Before he enter on the execution of his office, he shall take the following oath or affirmation:—"I do solemnly swear (or affirm) that I will faithfully execute the office of President of the United States, and will to the best of my ability, preserve, protect and defend the Constitution of the United States."

Section 2

1. The President shall be commander in chief of the army and navy of the United States, and of the militia of the several States,

---

[7]Superseded by the Twelfth Amendment.
[8]See the Twentieth Amendment and the Twenty-fifth Amendment.

when called into the actual service of the United States; he may require the opinion, in writing, of the principal officer in each of the executive departments, upon any subject relating to the duties of their respective offices, and he shall have power to grant reprieves and pardons for offences against the United States, except in cases of impeachment.

2. He shall have power, by and with the advice and consent of the Senate, to make treaties, provided two-thirds of the senators present concur; and he shall nominate, and by and with the advice and consent of the Senate, shall appoint ambassadors, other public ministers and consuls, judges of the Supreme Court, and all other officers of the United States, whose appointments are not herein otherwise provided for, and which shall be established by law; but the Congress may by law vest the appointment of such inferior officers, as they think proper, in the President alone, in the courts of law, or in the heads of departments.

3. The President shall have power to fill up all vacancies that may happen during the recess of the Senate, by granting commissions which shall expire at the end of the next session.

Section 3

1. He shall from time to time give to the Congress information of the state of the Union, and recommend to their consideration such measures as he shall judge necessary and expedient; he may, on extraordinary occasions, convene both Houses, or either of them, and in case of disagreement between them with respect to the time of adjournment, he may adjourn them to such time as he shall think proper; he shall receive ambassadors and other public ministers; he shall take care that the laws be faithfully executed, and shall commission all the officers of the United States.

Section 4

The President, Vice President, and all civil officers of the United States, shall be removed from office on impeachment for, and conviction of, treason, bribery, or other high crimes and misdemeanors.

Article III

Section 1

The Judicial power of the United States shall be vested in one Supreme Court, and in such inferior courts as the Congress may from time to time ordain and establish. The judges, both of the Supreme and inferior courts, shall hold their offices during good behavior, and shall, at stated times, receive for their services, a compensation, which shall not be diminished during their continuance in office.

Section 2

1. The Judicial power shall extend to all cases, in law and equity, arising under this Constitution, the laws of the United States, and treaties made, or which shall be made, under their authority;—to all cases affecting ambassadors, other public ministers and consuls;—to all cases of admiralty and maritime jurisdiction;—to controversies to which the United States shall be a party;—to controversies between two or more States, between a State and citizens of another State,[9] between citizens of different States, between citizens of the same State claiming lands under grants of different States, and between a State, or the citizens thereof, and foreign States, citizens or subjects.

2. In all cases affecting ambassadors, other public ministers and consuls, and those in which a State shall be party, the Supreme Court shall have original jurisdiction. In all the other cases before mentioned, the Supreme Court shall have appellate jurisdiction, both as to law and fact, with such exceptions, and under such regulations as the Congress shall make.

3. The trial of all crimes, except in cases of impeachment, shall be by jury; and such trial shall be held in the State where the said crimes shall have been committed; but when not committed within any State, the trial shall be at such place or places as the Congress may by law have directed.

Section 3

1. Treason against the United States shall consist only in levying war against them, or in adhering to their enemies, giving them aid and comfort. No person shall be convicted of treason unless on the testimony of two witnesses to the same overt act, or on confession in open court.

2. The Congress shall have power to declare the punishment of treason, but no attainder of treason shall work corruption of blood, or forfeiture except during the life of the person attained.

[9]See the Eleventh Amendment.

Article IV

Section 1

Full faith and credit shall be given in each State to the public acts, records, and judicial proceedings of every other State. And the Congress may by general laws prescribe the manner in which such acts, records and proceedings shall be proved, and the effect thereof.

Section 2

1. The citizens of each State shall be entitled to all privileges and immunities of citizens in the several States.

2. A person charged in any State with treason, felony, or other crime, who shall flee from justice, and be found in another State, shall on demand of the executive authority of the State from which he fled, be delivered up, to be removed to the State having jurisdiction of the crime.

3. No person held to service or labor in one State under the laws thereof, escaping into another, shall, in consequence of any law or regulation therein, be discharged from such service or labor, but shall be delivered up on claim of the party to whom such service or labor may be due.

Section 3

1. New States may be admitted by the Congress into this Union; but no new State shall be formed or erected within the jurisdiction of any other State; nor any State be formed by the junction of two or more States, or parts of States, without the consent of the legislatures of the States concerned as well as of the Congress.

2. The Congress shall have power to dispose of and make all needful rules and regulations respecting the territory or other property belonging to the United States; and nothing in this Constitution shall be so construed as to prejudice any claims of the United States, or of any particular State.

Section 4

The United States shall guarantee to every State in this Union a republican form of government, and shall protect each of them against invasion; and on application of the legislature, or of the executive (when the legislature cannot be convened) against domestic violence.

Article V

The Congress, whenever two-thirds of both Houses shall deem it necessary, shall propose amendments to this Constitution, or, on the application of the legislatures of two-thirds of the several States, shall call a convention for proposing amendments, which, in either case, shall be valid to all intents and purposes, as part of this Constitution, when ratified by the legislatures of three-fourths of the several States, or by conventions in three-fourths thereof, as the one or the other mode of ratification may be proposed by the Congress; Provided that no amendment which may be made prior to the year one thousand eight hundred and eight shall in any manner affect the first and fourth clauses in the ninth section of the first article; and that no State, without its consent, shall be deprived of its equal suffrage in the Senate.

Article VI

1. All debts contracted, and engagements entered into, before the adoption of this Constitution, shall be as valid against the United States under this Constitution, as under the Confederation.
2. This Constitution, and the laws of the United States which shall be made in pursuance thereof; and all treaties made, or which shall be made, under the authority of the United States, shall be the supreme law of the land; and the Judges in every State shall be bound thereby, anything in the Constitution or laws of any State to the contrary notwithstanding.
3. The senators and representatives before mentioned, and the members of the several State legislatures, and all executive and judicial officers, both of the United States and of the several States, shall be bound by oath or affirmation to support this Constitution; but no religious test shall ever be required as a qualification to any office or public trust under the United States.

Article VII

The ratification of the conventions of nine States shall be sufficient for the establishment of this Constitution between the States so ratifying the same.

Done in Convention, by the unanimous consent of the States present, the seventeenth day of September, in the year of our Lord one thousand seven hundred and eighty-seven, and of the indepen-

dence of the United States of America the twelfth. In witness whereof we have hereunto subscribed our names.
[Names omitted]

Articles in Addition To, and Amendment Of, the Constitution of the United States of America, Proposed by Congress, and Ratified by the Legislatures of the Several States, Pursuant to the Fifth Article of the Original Constitution.[10] *(The first ten amendments were ratified December 15, 1791, and form what is known as the "Bill of Rights.")*

Amendment 1

Congress shall make no law respecting an establishment of religion, or prohibiting the free exercise thereof; or abridging the freedom of speech, or of the press; or the right of the people peaceably to assemble, and to petition the Government for a redress of grievances.

Amendment 2

A well regulated Militia, being necessary to the security of a free State, the right of the people to keep and bear Arms, shall not be infringed.

Amendment 3

No Soldier shall, in time of peace be quartered in any house, without the consent of the Owner, nor in time of war, but in a manner to be prescribed by law.

Amendment 4

The right of the people to be secure in their persons, houses, papers, and effects, against unreasonable searches and seizures, shall not be violated, and no Warrants shall issue, but upon probable cause, supported by Oath or affirmation, and particularly describing the place to be searched, and the persons or things to be seized.

Amendment 5

No person shall be held to answer for a capital, or otherwise infamous crime, unless on a presentment or indictment of a Grand Jury,

[10]The Twenty-first Amendment was not ratified by state legislatures but by state conventions summoned by Congress.

except in cases arising in the land or naval forces, or in the Militia, when in actual service in time of War or public danger; nor shall any person be subject for the same offence to be twice put in jeopardy of life or limb; nor shall be compelled in any criminal case to be a witness against himself, nor be deprived of life, liberty, or property, without due process of law; nor shall private property be taken for public use, without just compensation.

Amendment 6

In all criminal prosecutions, the accused shall enjoy the right to a speedy and public trial, by an impartial jury of the State and district wherein the crime shall have been committed, which district shall have been previously ascertained by law, and to be informed of the nature and cause of the accusation; to be confronted with the witnesses against him; to have compulsory process for obtaining witnesses in his favor, and to have the Assistance of Counsel for his defense.

Amendment 7

In suits at common law, where the value in controversy shall exceed twenty dollars, the right of trial by jury shall be preserved, and no fact tried by a jury, shall be otherwise reexamined in any Court of the United States, than according to the rules of the common law.

Amendment 8

Excessive bail shall not be required, nor excessive fines imposed, nor cruel and unusual punishments inflicted.

Amendment 9

The enumeration in the Constitution, of certain rights, shall not be construed to deny or disparage others retained by the people.

Amendment 10

The powers not delegated to the United States by the Constitution, nor prohibited by it to the States, are reserved to the States respectively, or to the people.

Amendment 11
(Ratified February 7, 1795)

The Judicial power of the United States shall not be construed to extend to any suit in law or equity, commenced or prosecuted against one of the United States by Citizens of another State, or by Citizens or Subjects of any Foreign State.

Amendment 12
(Ratified July 27, 1804)

The Electors shall meet in their respective states and vote by ballot for President and Vice President, one of whom, at least, shall not be an inhabitant of the same state with themselves; they shall name in their ballots the person voted for as President, and in distinct ballots the person voted for as Vice President, and they shall make distinct lists of all persons voted for as President, and of all persons voted for as Vice President, and of the number of votes for each, which lists they shall sign and certify, and transmit sealed to the seat of the government of the United States, directed to the President of the Senate;—the President of the Senate shall, in presence of the Senate and House of Representatives, open all the certificates and the votes shall then be counted;—The person having the greatest number of votes for President, shall be the President, if such number be a majority of the whole number of Electors appointed; and if no person have such majority, then from the persons having the highest numbers not exceeding three on the list of those voted for as President, the House of Representatives shall choose immediately, by ballot, the President. But in choosing the President, the votes shall be taken by states, the representation from each state having one vote; a quorum for this purpose shall consist of a member or members from two-thirds of the states, and a majority of all the states shall be necessary to a choice. [And if the House of Representatives shall not choose a President whenever the right of choice shall devolve upon them, before the fourth day of March next following, then the Vice President shall act as President, as in the case of the death or other constitutional disability of the President.—][11] The person having the greatest number of votes as Vice President, shall be the Vice President, if such number be a majority of the whole number of Electors appointed, and if no person have a majority, then from the two

[11]Superseded by Section 3 of the Twentieth Amendment.

highest numbers on the list, the Senate shall choose the Vice President; a quorum for the purpose shall consist of two-thirds of the whole number of Senators, and a majority of the whole number shall be necessary to a choice. But no person constitutionally ineligible to the office of President shall be eligible to that of Vice President of the United States.

Amendment 13
(Ratified December 6, 1865)

Section 1

Neither slavery nor involuntary servitude, except as a punishment for crime whereof the party shall have been duly convicted, shall exist within the United States, or any place subject to their jurisdiction.

Section 2

Congress shall have power to enforce this article by appropriate legislation.

Amendment 14
(Ratified July 9, 1868)

Section 1

All persons born or naturalized in the United States, and subject to the jurisdiction thereof, are citizens of the United States and of the State wherein they reside. No State shall make or enforce any law which shall abridge the privileges or immunities of citizens of the United States; nor shall any State deprive any person of life, liberty, or property, without due process of law; nor deny to any person within its jurisdiction the equal protection of the laws.

Section 2

Representatives shall be apportioned among the several States according to their respective numbers, counting the whole number of persons in each State, excluding Indians not taxed. But when the right to vote at any election for the choice of electors for President and Vice President of the United States, Representatives in Congress, the Executive and Judicial officers of a State, or the members of the Legislature thereof, is denied to any of the male inhabitants of such

State, being twenty-one years of age,[12] and citizens of the United States, or in any way abridged, except for participation in rebellion, or other crime, the basis of representation therein shall be reduced in the proportion which the number of such male citizens shall bear to the whole number of male citizens twenty-one years of age in such State.

Section 3

No person shall be a Senator or Representative in Congress, or elector of President and Vice President, or hold any office, civil or military, under the United States, or under any State, who, having previously taken an oath, as a member of Congress, or as an officer of the United States, or as a member of any State legislature, or as an executive or judicial officer of any State, to support the Constitution of the United States, shall have engaged in insurrection or rebellion against the same, or given aid or comfort to the enemies thereof. But Congress may by a vote of two-thirds of each House, remove such disability.

Section 4

The validity of the public debt of the United States, authorized by law, including debts incurred for payment of pensions and bounties for services in suppressing insurrection or rebellion, shall not be questioned. But neither the United States nor any State shall assume or pay any debt or obligation incurred in aid of insurrection or rebellion against the United States, or any claim for the loss or emancipation of any slave; but all such debts, obligations and claims shall be held illegal and void.

Section 5

The Congress shall have power to enforce, by appropriate legislation, the provisions of this article.

Amendment 15
(Ratified February 3, 1870)

Section 1

The right of citizens of the United States to vote shall not be denied or abridged by the United States or by any State on account of race, color, or previous condition of servitude.

[12]Changed by Section 1 of the Twenty-sixth Amendment.

Section 2

The Congress shall have power to enforce this article by appropriate legislation.

Amendment 16
(Ratified February 3, 1913)

The Congress shall have power to lay and collect taxes on incomes, from whatever source derived, without apportionment among the several States, and without regard to any census or enumeration.

Amendment 17
(Ratified April 8, 1913)

The Senate of the United States shall be composed of two Senators from each State, elected by the people thereof, for six years; and each Senator shall have one vote. The electors in each State shall have the qualifications requisite for electors of the most numerous branch of the State legislatures.

When vacancies happen in the representation of any State in the Senate, the executive authority of such State shall issue writs of election to fill such vacancies; *Provided,* That the legislature of any State may empower the executive thereof to make temporary appointments until the people fill the vacancies by election as the legislature may direct.

This amendment shall not be so construed as to affect the election or term of any Senator chosen before it becomes valid as part of the Constitution.

Amendment 18
(Ratified January 16, 1919)

Section 1

After one year from the ratification of this article the manufacture, sale, or transportation of intoxicating liquors within, the importation thereof into, or the exportation thereof from the United States and all territory subject to the jurisdiction thereof for beverage purposes is hereby prohibited.

Section 2

The Congress and the several States shall have concurrent power to enforce this article by appropriate legislation.

Section 3

This article shall be inoperative unless it shall have been ratified as an amendment to the Constitution by the legislatures of the several States as provided in the Constitution, within seven years from the date of the submission hereof to the States by the Congress.[13]

Amendment 19
(Ratified August 18, 1920)

The right of citizens of the United States to vote shall not be denied or abridged by the United States or by any State on account of sex.

Congress shall have power to enforce this article by appropriate legislation.

Amendment 20
(Ratified January 23, 1933)

Section 1

The terms of the President and Vice President shall end at noon on the 20th day of January, and the terms of Senators and Representatives at noon on the 3d day of January, of the years in which such terms would have ended if this article had not been ratified; and the terms of their successors shall then begin.

Section 2

The Congress shall assemble at least once in every year, and such meeting shall begin at noon on the 3d day of January, unless they shall by law appoint a different day.

Section 3

If, at the time fixed for the beginning of the term of the President, the President elect shall have died, the Vice President elect shall become President. If a President shall not have been chosen before

[13]Repealed by Section 1 of the Twenty-first Amendment.

the time fixed for the beginning of his term, or if the President elect shall have failed to qualify, then the Vice President elect shall act as President until a President shall have qualified; and the Congress may by law provide for the case wherein neither a President elect nor a Vice President elect shall have qualified, declaring who shall then act as President, or the manner in which one who is to act shall be selected, and such person shall act accordingly until a President or Vice President shall have qualified.

Section 4

The Congress may by law provide for the case of the death of any of the persons from whom the House of Representatives may choose a President whenever the right of choice shall have devolved upon them, and for the case of the death of any of the persons from whom the Senate may choose a Vice President whenever the right of choice shall have devolved upon them.

Section 5

Sections 1 and 2 shall take effect on the 15th day of October following the ratification of this article.

Section 6

This article shall be inoperative unless it shall have been ratified as an amendment to the Constitution by the legislatures of three-fourths of the several States within seven years from the date of its submission.

Amendment 21
(Ratified December 5, 1933)

Section 1

The eighteenth article of amendment to the Constitution of the United States is hereby repealed.

Section 2

The transportation or importation into any State, Territory, or possession of the United States for delivery or use therein of intoxicating liquors, in violation of the laws thereof, is hereby prohibited.

Section 3

This article shall be inoperative unless it shall have been ratified as an amendment to the Constitution by conventions in the several States, as provided in the Constitution, within seven years from the date of the submission hereof to the States by the Congress.

Amendment 22
(Ratified February 27, 1951)

Section 1

No person shall be elected to the office of the President more than twice, and no person who has held the office of President, or acted as President, for more than two years of a term to which some other person was elected President shall be elected to the office of the President more than once. But this Article shall not apply to any person holding the office of President when this Article was proposed by the Congress, and shall not prevent any person who may be holding the office of President, or acting as President, during the term within which this Article becomes operative from holding the office of President or acting as President during the remainder of such term.

Section 2

This article shall be inoperative unless it shall have been ratified as an amendment to the Constitution by the legislatures of three-fourths of the several States within seven years from the date of its submission to the States by the Congress.

Amendment 23
(Ratified March 29, 1961)

Section 1

The District constituting the seat of Government of the United States shall appoint in such manner as the Congress may direct:

A number of electors of President and Vice President equal to the whole number of Senators and Representatives in Congress to which the District would be entitled if it were a State, but in no event more than the least populous State; they shall be in addition to those appointed by the States, but they shall be considered, for the purposes of the election of President and Vice President, to be electors appointed by a State; and they shall meet in the District and perform such duties as provided by the twelfth article of amendment.

Section 2

The Congress shall have power to enforce this article by appropriate legislation.

Amendment 24
(Ratified January 23, 1964)

Section 1

The right of citizens of the United States to vote in any primary or other election for President or Vice President, for electors for President or Vice President, or for Senator or Representative in Congress, shall not be denied or abridged by the United States or any State by reason of failure to pay any poll tax or other tax.

Section 2

The Congress shall have power to enforce this article by appropriate legislation.

Amendment 25
(Ratified February 10, 1967)

Section 1

In case of the removal of the President from office or of his death or resignation, the Vice President shall become President.

Section 2

Whenever there is a vacancy in the office of the Vice President, the President shall nominate a Vice President who shall take office upon confirmation by a majority vote of both Houses of Congress.

Section 3

Whenever the President transmits to the President pro tempore of the Senate and the Speaker of the House of Representatives his written declaration that he is unable to discharge the powers and duties of his office, and until he transmits to them a written declaration to the contrary, such powers and duties shall be discharged by the Vice President as Acting President.

Section 4

Whenever the Vice President and a majority of either the principal officers of the executive departments or of such other body as Congress may by law provide, transmit to the President pro tempore of the Senate and the Speaker of the House of Representatives their written declaration that the President is unable to discharge the powers and duties of his office, the Vice President shall immediately assume the powers and duties of the office as Acting President.

Thereafter, when the President transmits to the President pro tempore of the Senate and the Speaker of the House of Representatives his written declaration that no inability exists, he shall resume the powers and duties of his office unless the Vice President and a majority of either the principal officers of the executive department or of such other body as Congress may by law provide, transmit within four days to the President pro tempore of the Senate and the Speaker of the House of Representatives their written declaration that the President is unable to discharge the powers and duties of his office. Thereupon Congress shall decide the issue, assembling within forty-eight hours for that purpose if not in session. If the Congress, within twenty-one days after receipt of the latter written declaration, or, if Congress is not in session, within twenty-one days after Congress is required to assemble, determines by two-thirds vote of both Houses that the President is unable to discharge the powers and duties of his office, the Vice President shall continue to discharge the same as Acting President; otherwise, the President shall resume the powers and duties of his office.

Amendment 26
(Ratified July 1, 1971)

Section 1

The right of citizens of the United States, who are eighteen years of age or older, to vote shall not be denied or abridged by the United States or by any State on account of age.

Section 2

The Congress shall have the power to enforce this article by appropriate legislation.

Index